"*Peripheral Vision* should be required reading in any course on innovation designed for senior leaders. The concepts presented in this book have received outstanding feedback from our leaders and have unquestionably improved their critical thinking skills and significantly expanded their peripheral vision."

— John Allison, Chairman and CEO, BB&T Corporation

"As new technologies and competitors arise, managers and companies must cultivate new ways in which to read the weak signals on the periphery. This book offers a bold, imaginative, and practical process for redesigning how we sense, sift through, and respond to the many threats and opportunities around us."

— Larry Huston, Vice President, Innovation and Knowledge,
   The Procter & Gamble Company

"Today's managers live with the continual discomfort of knowing that threats and opportunities from the most unexpected places can blindside them at any moment. Day and Schoemaker have produced the first comprehensive framework to alleviate this anxiety. Written in a simple, logical, and actionable manner, this badly needed book provides a systematic way to expand the work of strategic thinking beyond the traditional models."

— Sanjiv Mirchandani, Executive Vice President,
   Fidelity Investments

"Day and Schoemaker's framework for *Peripheral Vision* is revolutionary, not only because it uncovers the causes of organizational paralysis but more so because it provides a simple methodology and a tool set to eliminate corporate tunnel vision. This is precisely the 'do-it-yourself' toolkit business leaders need to manage the 'enigma of the unknown.' The book provides an excellent survey for self-diagnosis and offers practical advice on how to strengthen critical organizational capability so you will not get blindsided again. This is extremely relevant for leaders of organizations in a maintenance mode as well as those involved in start-ups and emerging markets. It is a must-read for developing leaders of the future."

— **Govi Rao**, Vice President and General Manager, Solid State Lighting, Philips Electronics

"All business leaders know that focus and execution are critical; *Peripheral Vision* provides unique insight into how to mine your organization for great opportunities that lie just outside your focus."

— **Ted Mathas**, Executive Vice President, U.S. Insurance Operations, New York Life Insurance Company

# PERIPHERAL VISION

George S. Day
Paul J. H. Schoemaker

# PERIPHERAL VISION

## Detecting the Weak Signals That Will
## Make or Break Your Company

Harvard Business School Press

*Boston, Massachusetts*

*To my family, who sustain Marilyn's legacy.*
—George Day

*To Joyce with her keen eye for the periphery.*
—Paul Schoemaker

**Library of Congress Cataloging-in-Publication Data**
Day, George S.
    Peripheral vision : seven steps to seeing business opportunities sooner /
George S. Day, Paul J.H. Schoemaker.
      p. cm.
    ISBN 1-4221-0154-1
    1. Marketing—Management. 2. New products. 3. Strategic planning.
4. Industrial management. I. Schoemaker, Paul J. H. II. Title.
    HF5415.13D369 2006
    658.4'012—dc22

                                                            2005030884

# Contents

# Seven Steps to Bridging the Vigilance Gap

VEN AS YOU FOCUS on running your business, you face a barrage of weak signals from the periphery. Your sales manager in the Asia-Pacific region might pass along a disturbing rumor about a new competitor. Or you read in the paper that a few pioneers have implanted radio-frequency identification (RFID) tags under their skin to broadcast their ID and medical data in case of emergency. Perhaps you learn that the Web log (blog) of an aggrieved customer is attracting attention. What could these signals mean for your business? Which of the many weak signals around you deserve closer attention? Which ones can you safely ignore? With this growing complexity and increasing speed of change, a capacity for peripheral vision is crucial to success, and even survival. Yet the periphery, by its nature, lacks clarity. It is uncertain and capricious. The key is to quickly spot those signals that are relevant and explore them further, filter out the noise, and pursue opportunities ahead of the competition or recognize the early signs of trouble before they escalate into major problems. Is your organization up to this task?

Most organizations lack the requisite peripheral vision. More than 80 percent of the global senior executives who took the Strategic Eye Exam developed for this project felt that their capacity for peripheral vision would not meet their need. This shortfall manifests itself in a vigilance gap. How vigilant is your organization? That is, how many times have you been surprised by high-impact events in the past five years? A survey of 140 corporate strategists found that fully two-thirds admitted that their organizations had been surprised by as many as *three* high-impact competitive events in the past five years. Moreover, 97 percent of respondents said their companies lacked any early warning system to prevent such surprises in the future.[1]

While the eyes of individuals have a highly developed system for peripheral vision, most organizations are designed to be narrowly focused on the task at hand. This strong focus of attention may benefit short-term performance but may work against the organization's long-term survival, particularly when the environment changes. The weak signals that should be noticed may be obscured by irrelevant and distracting noise. If one person at the edge of an organization senses the significance of an early warning signal, will the rest of the organization receive or understand it? Take any of your past surprises; probably someone in your organization or extended network knew about it. But you didn't know that they knew; and they didn't know that you needed to know. Good peripheral vision is much more than sensing; it is also knowing where to look more carefully, knowing how to interpret the weak signals, and knowing how to act when the signals are still ambiguous.

In a highly connected world, faint stirrings can have large repercussions—from pharmaceutical executives who have been surprised by the growing unpopularity of their industry to manufacturers disrupted by low-cost rivals from China and India to the many Internet service providers who failed to see the potential of online search engines until Google outflanked them. What may first appear as a small concern at the periphery can quickly become a central concern. These cases are all too common. They can lead to tragic consequences such as the 9/11 terrorist attacks in the United States or to more positive, totally new insights such as Fleming's discovery of penicillin.

## Our Approach to Developing Peripheral Vision

This book began with the challenge: How can managers and their organizations build a superior capacity to recognize and act on weak signals from the periphery before it is too late? We initially sought answers as part of our research on emerging technologies at the Wharton School's Mack Center for Technological Innovation. In May 2003, we brought together a distinguished group of thought leaders for a conference on Peripheral Vision.[2] This conference, and a subsequent special issue of *Long Range Planning*, sharpened our thinking on this topic and raised important new questions. In these explorations, we found that the metaphor of peripheral vision was a powerful lens for understanding the complex and often confusing fuzzy zone at the edge of an organization.

Using the vision metaphor, this book draws on our own research into best practice as well as "next practice" in peripheral vision. We look at specific cases of success and failure in seeing changes at the periphery—from how Tasty Baking clarified the confusing signals about low-carb foods, to how Bratz dolls recognized changing attitudes in young girls to topple Barbie from her throne, to how funeral directors responded to a demand for more personalized services, to the challenges facing the lighting industry from the rise of light-emitting diode (LED) lighting. We draw on insights from the fields of strategy, marketing, organizational theory, innovation and emerging technology management, behavioral decision theory, and cognitive science, along with applied areas such as technology scanning, competitive intelligence, and marketing research. Finally, we include our diagnostic exam so you can assess your own organization's need for peripheral vision as well as its current capability (see appendix A).

To help improve peripheral vision, we especially examined underlying organizational processes and capabilities. Our approach draws on general models of information processing and organizational learning (see appendix B) but with a specific focus on the blurry and uncertain signals from the periphery. This led us to a seven-step process for understanding and enhancing peripheral vision, as summarized in figure I-1.

The first five steps focus on directly improving the process of receiving, interpreting, and acting on weak signals from the periphery. The first step, scoping, concerns how widely to look and what issues to address (chapter 2). To see everything is to see nothing. Managers can use a set of guiding questions to ensure that their focus is neither too broad nor too narrow, and avoid being overwhelmed or missing important parts of the picture. After the initial scope is determined, the next step is how to scan within the selected areas (chapter 3). Should the scanning focus more on the exploitation of a reasonably familiar domain or on the exploration of the unknown? To peer into new areas of the periphery, managers must employ different scanning strategies. Chapter 3 offers tools and approaches for detecting signals in different parts of the periphery, including inside the firm, customers and competitors, emerging technologies, and influencers and shapers. How should managers scan within the agreed scope?

Once the organization is scanning within a promising area, the next step is to make sense of what is found (chapter 4). Much of the information is ambiguous and incomplete. In human vision, signals at the periphery lack color or definition. How does the organization connect the dots to draw together and interpret the glimpses that it has

**FIGURE I-1**

## Seven steps to bridge the vigilance gap

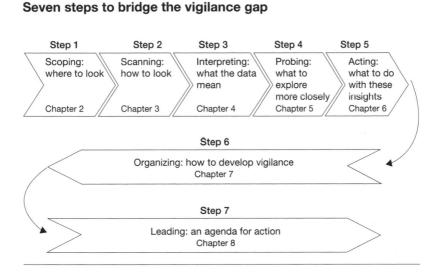

gathered from the periphery? What cognitive and organizational biases may get in the way? Among other strategies, the interpretation of
weak signals can be strengthened through diverse viewpoints—similar to the process of triangulation—to add depth and perspective.

Based on this preliminary interpretation, the next step is to
probe further to learn more about the periphery and develop a better view (chapter 5). This requires formulating good hypotheses and
knowing how to test them to confirm (as well as disconfirm) them.
Next, the organization must decide whether and how to act on the
signals from the periphery (chapter 6). Sometimes, the nature of the
threat or opportunity requires decisive action, even in the face of
high uncertainty. But often the ambiguous signals from the periphery require a more cautious and measured response using a real-
options perspective.

While steps 1 through 5 focus on improving the process of
peripheral vision, the last two steps focus on building broader organizational capabilities and leadership to support peripheral vision.

The seventh step makes the process an integral part of the organization's fabric and culture, helping to systematically hone the organizational capabilities needed in a truly vigilant organization (chapter 7). Finally, although everyone in the organization may play a role in peripheral vision, our survey clearly revealed the pivotal role that leaders play. How to develop leadership that fosters organizational curiosity is the challenge of the last step, and this is addressed in chapter 8. These last two steps inform and shape all the others.

## Anticipation and Alertness

The following chapters show you, step by step, how to apply these and other insights to improve the peripheral vision of your own organization. Among the important insights we have gained from our investigation of the periphery are:

- You must ask the right questions to identify what you don't know so that you can explore the edge of your business.

- You must balance active scanning with splatter vision (undirected searches) to probe deeply with these focusing questions.

- You often must identify new sources of information or new ways of scanning to unveil important but hidden parts of the periphery.

- You can use "triangulation" with multiple methods to help clarify ambiguous signals and interpret fuzzy signals at the periphery.

- You often must actively prod and probe to learn more about especially promising or threatening signals.

- Although you must occasionally commit strongly, you may have to stay flexible with a sound portfolio of strategic options as well.

- Peripheral vision is a capability that any organization can develop and strengthen, just as people can.

- Superior peripheral vision requires leadership with strategic foresight that sets an example and encourages the sharing of insights and concerns.

Although our seven-step process can strengthen your organization's peripheral vision, keep in mind that there is nothing simple about the periphery. Effective peripheral vision does *not* boil down to a standard, linear recipe. It requires practice, dedication, and seasoned judgment. Understanding the periphery is not so much about following a formula as it is about asking the right questions and reflecting on them appropriately. It is not about prediction but rather about anticipation and alertness. The book will deepen your strategic insight and encourage you to look beyond your present frames of reference. It will urge you to peek around your own organizational blinders. It is worth the effort. Superior peripheral vision can help you anticipate risks and see opportunities sooner while gaining a profitable advantage over your blinkered rivals.

# Chapter One

# The Periphery

## Why It Matters

*"When spring comes, snow melts first at the periphery, because that is where it is most exposed."*

—Andy Grove, Intel[1]

VINCE MELCHIORRE, senior vice president and chief marketing officer of Philadelphia-based Tasty Baking, had an epiphany in the aisle of a suburban supermarket. While he was looking over shelf displays, he was accosted by a woman in her sixties and her mother, who was in her eighties. The mother had diabetes and could no longer eat his company's beloved sweet snacks. "They were yelling at me in the store," Melchiorre recalled. "The mother had eaten Tastykakes since she was a child. She could still sing the jingle. They couldn't eat them anymore. They asked, 'Why aren't you doing anything about it?' It took me over the top."[2]

At the time, in early 2004, the low-carb revolution launched by Dr. Robert Atkins was in full swing. Every food company had a low-carb strategy and thousands of new products were being rolled out. A company such as Tasty Baking, which turned out more than 5 million cakes, pies, cookies, doughnuts, and other indulgent sweets each day under its Tastykake brand, couldn't fail to notice. Competitors such as Entenmann's were creating their own lines of low-carb products. But what did this trend really mean? Would the business dry up, or would low-carb diets be a passing fad? How quickly and in what way should Tasty Baking react?

At the time of Melchiorre's encounter in the supermarket aisle, Tasty Baking was well on its way to creating its own low-carb line, in a top-secret project that was code named "Greta" (short for "Greta Carbo," a pun on the screen actress's name). The company's new CEO, Charles Pizzi, pushed for the launch of an innovative new line as an integral part of reviving the company's sales, which had peaked at $166 million in 2001. The product team, led by Director of New Business Development Karen Schutz, raced to roll out the new low-carb product line by August 2004, cutting a process that typically takes twelve to eighteen months in half.

After his encounter with the women in the supermarket, however, Melchiorre came back with a new proposal for the team: shift the line from low-carb to sugar-free. This was by no means a simple proposition. The development team already had gone through many experimental batches of low-carb products to come up with products worthy of its brand. Changing the product line to sugar-free meant reformulating ingredients and retesting, almost like starting from scratch. "We were halfway down the road with the low-carb strategy," Melchiorre said. "It was not a happy day for me when I had to go in and see the people in product development and marketing."

But the picture had become crystal clear to Melchiorre. "I listened to people in stores, the people who stock the shelves and the consumers walking by. People were beating me up all the time because they love Tastykakes and couldn't eat them anymore because they are diabetic. I didn't get one person come up to me and say they couldn't eat them because they are on a low-carb diet. Carbs are important, but sugar is the bigger issue."

A former marketing executive at Campbell Soup, Melchiorre realized there was a difference between what people say and what they do. At Campbell Soup, he had been involved with sodium-free soups only to watch them fizzle. "People will say they want sodium-free or low-carb foods. Then they'll leave the focus group and go to McDonald's and supersize everything," said Melchiorre. "I've been in the food industry a long time. I've seen things come and go. The only way people get religion about these kinds of trends is when it affects them personally." His long experience colored the way he interpreted the news reports and other information he received.

Tasty Baking did formulate its line of sugar-free products, dubbed Tastykake Sensables, and launched it in August 2004. The products contained zero grams of sugar and only four to eight net grams of carbohydrates per serving. The line included plain and chocolate doughnuts, orange and chocolate-chip finger cakes, and cookie bars. It succeeded far beyond expectations, achieving sales that were double its targets. By the second quarter of 2005, the company's net route sales were up 8 percent over the previous year, driven in large part by the Sensables line.

But did Tasty Baking really make the right choice? As it turned out, Melchiorre had a chance to look down the road not taken. Around the same time that he was rolling out the sugar-free line, rival Entenmann's launched its low-carb line. As Melchiorre walked through supermarkets during the first few weeks, stores couldn't keep the Entenmann's product in stock. Had he made the right decision in focusing on sugar-free? But in the second and third months, he saw his hunch vindicated. Entenmann's low-carb products piled up. The line was eventually pulled, and Entenmann's launched its own sugar-free products. "A lot of companies have pulled their low-carb lines," he said. By May 2005, a *New York Times* article noting the transformation of many products from low-carb to low-sugar declared that "Low-sugar has become the new low-carb."[3] But many millions of dollars had been lost or gained in the meantime.

While the women in the supermarket aisle brought the picture into focus for Melchiorre, they were not his only source of information. In addition to walking the aisles of supermarkets about twice a week, Melchiorre reads widely and speaks with others in the industry. He bounces ideas off family and neighbors. He occasionally surveys the company's fifteen hundred employees. "We triangulate from a lot of different sources," he said. Once the company decided on the sugar-free strategy, Melchiorre also asked his trucking and operations people to serve as devil's advocates and identify what might go wrong so the company could hedge its bets if the product line failed and wouldn't be overcommitted.

Most of all, Melchiorre says, he tries to keep an open mind: "The biggest thing that I have seen most successful people do is to approach every day as a new learning experience. I put aside all my assumptions and go into today like I know nothing. What hurts people often is that they believe they know the answers and so they spend time trying to confirm their views. I never assume I have all of the answers. I'm always bouncing weird ideas off people—like what if we used our trucks to deliver tortilla shells or fruit? If you are trapped in your paradigm, you won't have good peripheral vision; you'll suffer from tunnel vision. Everyone follows everyone else, right off the plank."

## The Cost of Poor Peripheral Vision

One reason peripheral vision is so important is that companies often have a limited window in which to profit from a new insight at the periphery. Fashions go from Paris runways to Wal-Mart discount racks. Cell phones go from a high-priced business tool to an accessory in the pocket of every teenager. Arrive too early for the party and there are no guests; arrive too late and you are cleaning up the trash. Seeing what is happening and responding effectively is a key capability.

While Tasty Baking benefited from its peripheral vision, other industry segments were also trying to respond to the low-carb revolution. As Atkins and other low-carb diets raced across America like a brushfire, a significant market for low-carb foods emerged, producing $1.6 billion in sales in the first nine months of 2004. In 2003 and 2004, companies introduced a total of 3,737 low-carb products (most of which were variations on existing foods) in the United States alone.[4] Pioneers who recognized this gold rush early and acted effectively found fat profits in lean products. Sales of low-carb foods grew at triple-digit rates in 2003.

But then the trend hit a wall. Even as new product launches continued to rise, low-carb dieting began to fall. The percentage of Americans following Atkins and the low-carb South Beach diets plummeted from 9 percent in January 2004 to 4.6 percent nine months later, at the same time that the number of low-carb products doubled, as shown in figure 1-1. Companies that moved too slowly,

**FIGURE 1-1**

**Risk and reward at the periphery**

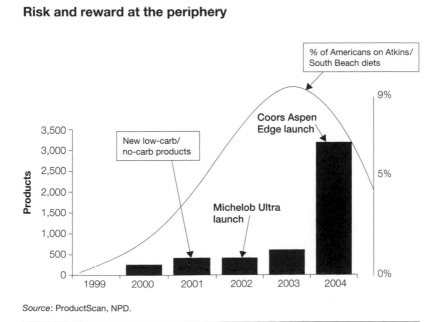

*Source*: ProductScan, NPD.

such as Coors, invested in product launches for a shrinking market crowded with products (see box, "Arriving at the Bar After Closing Time"). They missed the window of opportunity.

In hindsight, there were many signs of both the emergence and retrenchment of the low-carb diet revolution, some of which are illustrated in figure 1-2. Did companies see them? Did they recognize their significance amid all the other signals out there? Why couldn't

---

# Arriving at the Bar After Closing Time

Anheuser-Busch was one of the pioneers in the low-carb category in beer, launching Michelob Ultra in September 2002. It rapidly became the leader, capturing 5.7 percent of the light-beer market by March 2004. It was the company's most successful new brand launch since the introduction of Bud Light in 1982.[a] The company jumped on this wave early and rode the upsurge of the low-carb trend. Coors, in contrast, initially chose to wait for the low-carb fad to pass. It was not until Michelob Ultra began eroding the share for Coors Light that Coors launched its own low-carb brand in March 2004—eighteen months behind Anheuser-Busch. The new Coors brand, Aspen Edge, was too little, too late, despite the company's $30 million investment in the launch. Sales peaked at just 0.4 percent of the beer market in July 2004 before sliding downward. (A survey of distributors by analysts in September 2004 found that 87 percent did not believe the Aspen Edge brand would *ever* be successful.) By the time Coors recognized and acted on the low-carb fad, the window of opportunity had closed.

a. Anheuser-Busch 2003 Annual Report, 3.

FIGURE 1-2

## Some signals of the rise and fall of low-carb diets

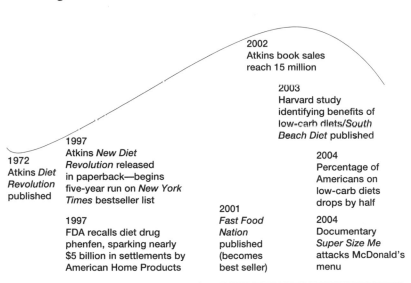

2002
Atkins book sales
reach 15 million

2003
Harvard study
identifying benefits of
low-carb diets/*South
Beach Diet* published

1997
Atkins *New Diet
Revolution* released
in paperback—begins
five-year run on *New York
Times* bestseller list

1972
Atkins *Diet
Revolution*
published

2004
Percentage of
Americans on
low-carb diets
drops by half

2001
*Fast Food
Nation*
published
(becomes
best seller)

1997
FDA recalls diet drug
phenfen, sparking nearly
$5 billion in settlements by
American Home Products

2004
Documentary
*Super Size Me*
attacks McDonald's
menu

they respond effectively? The problem with signals from the periphery is that they are often faint and ambiguous. In the case of low-carb foods, for example, the picture was made blurry by the complexities and vagaries of consumer behavior. Individuals often developed their own definitions of low-carb diets. A 2004 study by the Hartman Group found that only 9 percent of those on low-carb diets were strictly following them. The study also found that the percentage of consumers on their own low-carb diets exceeded the percentages on every formal low-carb plan. In addition, there was rapid churn. Of the 34 percent of dieters who had tried a low-carb diet, more than half had dropped the diet by the end of the first year, similar to other diets. For most dieters, focused interest in a low-carb diet lasted about three months.[5]

How this dieting translated into buying behavior was even more complicated. The Hartman Group found, for example, that while low-carb dieting demonized certain foods (such as French fries and pasta), consumers were not cutting back on the use of their old brands in favor of new low-carb brands. The picture was blurry in every way, yet companies such as Tasty Baking had to act quickly. So, how can companies better develop their peripheral vision so that they see sooner and respond more effectively to weak signals in the environment?

## The Vigilance Gap

Most organizations do not have a sufficient capability for peripheral vision. Our survey of more than 150 global senior managers found that over 80 percent said that their company's capability for peripheral vision falls short of what they will need, resulting in a significant vigilance gap.[6] The average expected need for peripheral vision was above 5 on a 7-point scale, while the mean capacity was at 4, as illustrated in figure 1-3. (How does your organization stack up? To assess the gap in your own organization, see the Strategic Eye Exam in appendix A.)

FIGURE 1-3

**The rising need for vigilance**

*Our survey of more than 150 senior executives found that their expected need for peripheral vision outstripped their current capacity, creating a vigilance gap.*

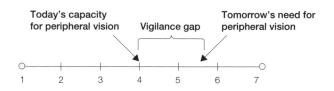

*Source*: Strategic Eye Exam survey of senior managers in the United States and Europe, 2004.

How much peripheral vision does an organization need? Organisms and organizations need senses that match the demands of their environments. For example, bees can detect ultraviolet light, which allows them to distinguish among varieties of white flowers, and some species of moths have evolved the capacity to detect the sonar of bats.[7] When the moth detects this sonar, it triggers an evasive dive. These moths cannot hear anything else, but they have developed a strong capability for this highly specialized perception. The danger is when the environment changes—for example, when a moth finds its way into a house and the threat is no longer a sonar-guided bat but rather a broom-wielding human. Then the moth's old capabilities for perception are no longer up to the task.

Similarly, the peripheral vision needed by an organization must be tailored to its strategy, the dynamics of its industry, and the volatility of its environment. Increased speed and complexity in the environment generally lead to a greater need for peripheral vision.[8] For example, in the past, companies in the $150 billion fashion industry could almost dictate which seasonal trends would be translated into clothes and then sell them in high volumes. But now, women are creating their own individual styles with a mix-and-match approach to wardrobe. This is part of a broader trend toward customization—from burning personalized tracks of music CDs to publishing blogs and podcasting online. Retailers are forced to revamp cookie-cutter stores to portray an image of uniqueness and customization. Fashion manufacturers have had to create flexible approaches such as the "quick draw" system used by Zara to offer greater, faster variety. These rapid changes cause much uncertainty and put a high premium on good peripheral vision to spot changes in markets and channels before others do.

Some companies have sufficient peripheral vision to meet the needs of their environment, as shown in figure 1-4. The focused company, with narrow vision in a relatively stable environment, is

**FIGURE 1-4**

### Peripheral vision and the environment

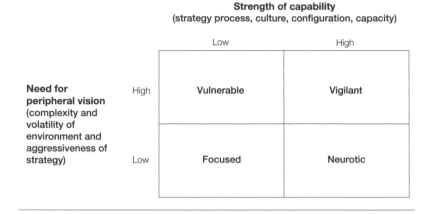

|  |  | Strength of capability (strategy process, culture, configuration, capacity) | |
|---|---|---|---|
|  |  | Low | High |
| Need for peripheral vision (complexity and volatility of environment and aggressiveness of strategy) | High | Vulnerable | Vigilant |
|  | Low | Focused | Neurotic |

like a race horse with blinders galloping forward on a clear, smooth track. The vigilant organization, with highly developed peripheral vision to deal with more chaotic environments, also has peripheral vision that is well matched to its environment. In contrast, some organizations have more peripheral vision than they need, leading to a neurotic organization that suffers from sensory overload. These organizations end up scanning everything, even though they are in a relatively placid environment, resulting in information overload and attention deficit—the organizational equivalent of children who have seizures while watching fast-moving television animation. This can make them less competitive than their more focused rivals.[9]

But the most common problem, based on our surveys, is the vulnerable organization, which has less peripheral vision than it needs to meet future demands. These organizations have a low capability for peripheral vision, even though they operate in an environment or pursue a strategy that demands a strong capacity for scanning the edges of the business. They tend to be myopic, concentrating on the business close at hand when many factors in the periphery could actually change their business model or industry. This particular mismatch results in missed opportunities and deadly blind spots, which have an impact not only on organizations but individual careers (see box, "These CEOs Never Saw It Coming"). Organizations in this quadrant must greatly enhance their capability for peripheral vision to match the challenges of their strategy and environment. This quadrant is the primary focus of our book.

## How Peripheral Vision Works

The metaphor of peripheral vision helps highlight the complex mechanisms underlying an organization's capability to see what lies around the corner. As with human and animal vision, the periphery is the fuzzy zone outside the area of primary focus (see box, "Central Versus Peripheral Viewing"). In human sight, focal vision helps us concentrate on core tasks such as reading or working on a project.[10]

# These CEOs Never Saw It Coming

How important is good peripheral vision to your career? When training company Leadership IQ asked 1,087 directors who had fired CEOs about what led to the pink slips, 31 percent said the CEOs had mismanaged change, 28 percent said they had ignored customers, 27 percent said they had tolerated low performers, and 23 percent said they were terminated for "denying reality."[a] In other words, poor peripheral vision contributed to most of these firings.

a. Jessi Hempel, "Why the Boss Really Had to Say Goodbye," *Business Week*, July 4, 2005, www.businessweek.com/magazine/content/05_27/c3941003_mz003.htm#ZZZTCY7OAAF.

# Central Versus Peripheral Viewing

Only a small focal area of the eye called the *fovea* (about the size of a thumbnail when our hand is stretched out) is used for central viewing at high resolution with full color. The periphery is scanned at a much lower resolution. The fovea offers the narrowest, but also sharpest, view of the world. Peripheral vision offers a wider, but increasingly fuzzy, view. In organizations, core internal activities and monitoring of the external environment, such as the data that is continuously examined by management or reported to investors, show up in the fovea (or focal area). How narrow or broad should this focal area be?

Peripheral vision helps us see the threats sneaking up on us or recognize the opportunities at the edges of our vision. In early human evolution, our peripheral vision helped us recognize the mountain lion about to spring or the deer moving through the woods that might provide dinner. Our peripheral vision continues to be vital in tasks such as driving or playing sports.

For organizations, as for individuals, what emerges at the periphery is difficult to see, tough to comprehend, and hard to seize or evade. In essence, peripheral vision requires different strategies and capabilities than focal vision in such areas as scoping, scanning, interpreting, probing, and acting. It entails much more than merely receiving a signal at the edge of vision. It is knowing where to look, how to look, what the signals mean, when to turn one's head to look in a new direction, and how to act on these ambiguous signals.

Vision involves an interplay between sensing and interpreting, so what we see is often determined by what we are prepared to see. Individuals and organizations can be so focused on a task that they fail to recognize a very significant change in the environment because it is outside of the focus of attention (see box, "They Didn't See the Gorilla").

# They Didn't See the Gorilla

We use a short video in our seminars to illustrate the special challenges of peripheral vision. The video shows players passing a basketball. Managers are asked to count how often players on a team with white shirts pass a basketball among themselves (they never pass to players in black shirts); at the same time, the black team is passing another ball around. As the managers count, someone dressed in a black gorilla suit walks slowly across the scene, without disturbing any of the players passing their basketballs. The gorilla stops in the middle, pounds his chest demonstrably, and then slowly leaves. Then we ask, How many times was the ball passed? About 90 percent get the count right. Next we ask, Did you happen to notice anything else? Hardly any managers notice the gorilla. Afterward, many demand a replay. When they clearly see the gorilla, some suspect we faked it and others stare in total disbelief. Individuals can fall victim to tunnel vision by focusing so intently on a task that they fail to see what is right in front of them.[a]

a. In a controlled experiment with college students, about 42 percent of subjects saw the gorilla; see Daniel J. Simons and Christopher F. Chabris, "Gorillas in Our Midst: Sustained Inattention Blindness for Dynamic Events," *Perception* 28 (1999): 1059–1074.

## Rods Versus Cones: Trade-offs at the Periphery

Given that the processes and capabilities for peripheral vision are different from those for focal vision, there is usually a cost involved in strengthening peripheral vision. Companies must commit resources as well as senior management attention to developing the necessary capabilities and processes to better sense weak signals at the periphery. This leads to a fundamental challenge for the organization: What is the right balance between focal and peripheral vision?

If you are constantly checking your side and rearview mirrors, you will decrease critical attention from the road ahead. Think of how AT&T took destructive and distractive forays into personal computers and other areas before divesting businesses deemed non-core. Sometimes, to see everything is to see nothing.

The human eye devotes considerable resources to peripheral vision, in the form of dedicated sensors. The eye contains two types of cells: rods and cones. The cone cells are concentrated near the center and allow us to see color and detail if lighting is good. This is where focal vision is concentrated. The rod cells, on the other hand, are located around the edges of the retina and are used in poor light or to see objects from the corner of your eye, such as a car overtaking you in the next lane on a highway.

The retina of the human eye has many more rod cells (for peripheral vision) than cone cells (for focal vision)—about 120 million rod cells compared with only 6 million cone cells. This ratio would not make sense if we were designing a robot to optimize performance in the task at hand—such as a machine designed to read books or count money. But the human eye is also designed to sense weak signals related to potential attacks or opportunities. How many organizations devote resources to peripheral versus focal vision at anywhere near a ratio of 20:1? We suspect that most organizations probably have the reverse ratio, as illustrated in figure 1-5, potentially resulting in myopia and tunnel vision.

FIGURE 1-5

## What is the right balance?

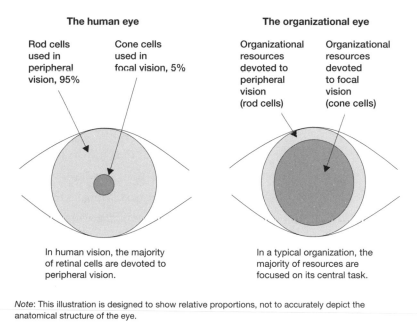

**The human eye**

Rod cells used in peripheral vision, 95%

Cone cells used in focal vision, 5%

In human vision, the majority of retinal cells are devoted to peripheral vision.

**The organizational eye**

Organizational resources devoted to peripheral vision (rod cells)

Organizational resources devoted to focal vision (cone cells)

In a typical organization, the majority of resources are focused on its central task.

*Note:* This illustration is designed to show relative proportions, not to accurately depict the anatomical structure of the eye.

# Improving Peripheral Vision

John McPhee's profile of U.S. Senator Bill Bradley's college basketball career describes his uncanny sense of awareness of other players around him on the court. For his article, McPhee took Bradley to an ophthalmologist to test his peripheral vision. It turned out that Bradley's peripheral vision was so highly developed that it was off the ophthalmologist's 180-degree scale. Bradley had a range of 195 degrees horizontally. While he may have been naturally gifted, he had also cultivated his peripheral vision. As a child, he used to walk down the sidewalk looking straight ahead while trying to identify items in the shop windows to the right or left. Later, he would stand at various places on the basketball court with his back to the basket, turn quickly, and try to shoot blind as the net appeared at his periphery. Bradley honed what McPhee described as a superb "sense of where you are."[11]

Many other athletes possess this highly developed ability to pay attention to the periphery, from the quarterback looking for a receiver while avoiding tacklers to a tennis player watching an opponent's movement while keeping an eye on the ball. In the midst of a complex and fast-changing field of play, they have a good sense of what is going on around them and know how to act quickly. Can organizations develop a similar capability to sense and respond to changes in their environments? We believe they can, and the remaining chapters of this book detail the organizational processes and capabilities that are needed to strengthen organizational peripheral vision.

In our survey of senior executives, the attitude of leadership toward the periphery came out as one of the most significant components of a capability for peripheral vision. Leaders define what the organization sees and apprehends. They also determine which voices are heard. Leadership at various levels either opens the organization to weak signals from the environment and inside the firm or shuts these signals out. Even an organization with the strongest individual mechanisms and processes for peripheral vision can find itself limited by a leader who squints or ignores all the weak signals that come in. Just think of poor Colonel Johann Gottlieb Rall in Trenton during the American Revolution, who died with an advance warning of George Washington's daring attack in his pocket. The signal had come in, but the leader, in the midst of holiday partying, had apparently ignored it.

Our research also found that a culture that encourages the sharing of information is essential to strong peripheral vision. Table 1-1 summarizes the organizational dimensions that matter most according to the statistical analysis of our survey.

**TABLE 1-1**

## Vulnerable versus vigilant organizations

|  | Vulnerable | Vigilant |
|---|---|---|
| Leadership | Narrowly focused on current performance and competitors | Focused on periphery and core |
| Strategy making | Rigid, static investments | Inquisitive, option oriented |
| Knowledge sharing | Focused on tracking pre-selected business data | Focused on gathering and sharing weak signals |
| Organizational configuration | Configured to look in (navel gazing) | Configured to look out (stargazing) |
| Culture | Rigid and conformist | Flexible and curious |

Like athletes such as Bill Bradley, who engage in exercises to strengthen their ability to scan the periphery, high-performing organizations can systematically improve their peripheral vision. They can become less vulnerable and more vigilant. The remaining chapters of the book examine how to do so.

# Chapter Two

# Scoping

## Where to Look

*"Judge a man by his questions*
*rather than his answers."*

—*Voltaire*

THE SYNDICATED MARKET data used by a major pet-food maker suggested that the firm was holding its dominant share in a flat market. This seemed to be good news. In reality, however, the company was losing share in a broader total market that was growing rapidly. The emergence of scientific pet food formulas sold through nontraditional specialty outlets and veterinarians was not reflected in the company's data. While managers were vaguely aware of this trend, they were looking too narrowly at their market so that the loss of their share of the total market did not show up in their market reports. They were losing ground and didn't even realize it. In trying to pinpoint why they had missed the early signals of the importance of this new segment, managers cited their own complacency in using readily available sales data from traditional channels. This set of blinders prevented the managers from seeing the bigger picture. The company ended up as a late and lackluster entrant in an already crowded market.

One of the first challenges of peripheral vision is determining how broadly to look. If the scope is too narrow, companies such as the pet-food manufacturer can be hit with surprises from outside their field of vision. But if the scope is too broad, the companies risk being overwhelmed with signals that are unimportant. How can companies define an appropriate scope for their vision to see everything that is important without wasting resources?

What is the right scope? This is one of those questions that doesn't lead directly to an answer—but rather to more questions. Defining scope has less to do with knowledge than curiosity. It hinges less on knowing the answers than on defining the right questions to reveal the limits of our current knowledge and then discovering where to look for answers. The pet-food maker might have asked, What new channels or business models might disrupt the industry? What is our share of the total market of pet owners? What is our share of wallet of individual customers? Because the managers failed to ask these questions, they were not able to see what was happening in their periphery until it became a major problem.

In this chapter, we examine a set of guiding questions that can break through a narrow scope and identify where to look for answers in the periphery. Asking and answering these questions can help direct the attention of managers to the parts of the periphery that might offer the greatest opportunities or pose the greatest threats.

# The Challenge of Scope

With blurring industry boundaries, establishing the correct scope is considerably more challenging. Companies in telecommunications and entertainment, for example, must contend with diverse players, such as video game designers and peer-to-peer exchange sites facilitating illegal downloads. Pharmaceutical companies increasingly must address the changing regulation of U.S. health care such as the new Medicare prescription drug coverage, as well as biotechnology breakthroughs and automated technologies for finding promising new compounds. Consumer products companies must address the rising Hispanic population in U.S. society through foods and flavors tailored to this growing segment.

These changes often start out far from the initial focal area of the company and gradually become an area of increasing attention. At what point do these emerging trends appear on the radar screen of companies? How do managers define the edges of the "known world" and thus the bounds of their periphery? Just as the eye tends to see most clearly in its central visual area, most organizations have a very distinct view of the focal business but an incomplete picture of everything else. New regulations, such as Sarbanes-Oxley for public companies, are directing even more of the attention of executives to monitoring and controlling the focal business. What opportunities might be missed as a result?

## The Dangers of Seeing Too Little or Too Much

Failures to recognize weak signals outside an organization's primary area of focus have resulted in missed opportunities for some organizations and created opportunities for others, as illustrated in table 2-1. Had makers of genetically modified food (GMO) additives asked, "What level of risk are consumers willing to tolerate in their

**TABLE 2-1**

## Opportunities in weak signals

| Domain | Opportunities in the periphery | Who saw it | Who missed it |
|---|---|---|---|
| Technological | Digital revolution | Apple and iPod | Music industry |
| | White LED lighting | LED companies | Lightbulb manufacturers |
| | Open-source software | Linux, IBM | Microsoft, Sun Microsystems |
| | CD-ROM encyclopedias | Microsoft | Encyclopedia Britannica |
| | Rapid spread of GSM (global system for mobile communications) | Nokia | Iridium |
| Economic | Overnight package delivery | FedEx, UPS | U.S. Postal Service, United Airlines |
| | Search engine potential | Google | Microsoft |
| | Discount point-to-point airlines | Southwest Airlines, Ryanair, EasyJet | United Airlines, Delta, Lufthansa |
| Societal | Sports and new age drinks | Snapple, Gatorade | Coca-Cola, PepsiCo (initially) |
| | Popularity of reality shows | Reality-show producers | Game-show producers |
| | Age compression and demand for more sophisticated dolls | MGA Entertainment (Bratz) | Mattel (Barbie) |
| Political | Generic AIDS drugs in Africa | Indian pharmaceutical companies | Major global pharmaceutical companies |
| | Social discontent in Venezuela | Hugo Chavez | Petróleos de Venezuela SA |
| | Role of exurbs in changing U.S. voter patterns | George Bush and Karl Rove | John Kerry |
| | Unmanned aerial vehicles (such as the drones used in Iraq) | Northrup-Grumman (via an acquisition) | Lockheed-Martin, Boeing |

food supply and how do they think about this?" they would have seen abundant signs that consumers were uneasy about trusting food manufacturers. Had drug makers in the United States asked, "How will patients and payers respond to increased advertising, shifts in health care systems, and the high costs of pharmaceuticals?" they would not have been as surprised at the sharp decline in public confidence.

On the other hand, with limited attention and other resources, companies that extend their scope too broadly can exhaust their resources. One study of senior executives, for example, concluded that performance actually decreased as accuracy of knowledge increased. A little knowledge may be a dangerous thing, but too much knowledge poses its own threats. Executives' desire to get more accurate market estimates led to wasted resources or even outright damage in some cases.[1] The challenge is to expand the scope just enough to include all the relevant parts of the environment but no further.

## Setting the Right Scope

In addition to adjusting to changes in the environment, the company should adjust its scope to the organization's strategic vision. When Abbott Laboratories recognized in the early 1960s that it would probably not become a leading pharmaceutical company, it expanded its scope to find peripheral growth opportunities. This scoping led the company successfully into diagnostic products, infant nutritionals, and hospital supplies. On the other hand, some companies, even in rapidly changing environments, elect to "stick to their knitting" and grow by edging carefully outward from their current scope. These companies will not need as broad a scope of peripheral vision—just enough to see into adjacent markets. For example, Dell Computers has sustained its remarkable growth by extending its "build to order" business model to similar markets such as printers and low-end servers. Meanwhile, Dell has paid careful attention to changes around this focal point, such as the integration of computing and entertainment, which may have a significant impact on its focal business.

## Asking the Right Questions

Effective scoping hinges on the ability to pose the right questions, and these questions are different from those related to the focal business, which can be very precise and targeted. Focal questions often become so routine that the answers can be gathered automatically and displayed in neat dashboards. What is our market share? What are our profits? Have our sales volumes increased? What is our employee turnover? What are rivals up to? Managers are usually very proficient (and sometimes neurotic) in asking and answering such questions.

But in the periphery, the best questions are much more open-ended. The answers are far less precise. What parts of the world are overlooked? What questions don't get answered because they are never posed? Where standard analysis focuses on the solid matter, the challenge of the periphery is to question the part of the picture that is *missing*. Some of these questions about the periphery may appear in the form of hypotheses, but many may not be so distinctly articulable. Sound scoping requires an open mind, tolerance for ambiguity, and the courage to venture into unfamiliar terrain. In the periphery, wrong questions could lead you on endless wild-goose chases. But a few good questions can help identify unseen opportunities. We consider some of these "thought starters" below; they are organized around learning from the past, amplifying the present, and anticipating the future. Asking and answering these questions can help to test whether the organization has the right scope.

## Learning from the Past

The past may not be a good predictor of the future, but it can point out persistent blind spots in your company or industry. It can also offer lessons from other industries that might apply to your own.

*What have been our past blind spots?* Start a few decades back and list systematically all the political, economic, social, and technological changes that occurred in and around your industry. Which ones did management miss that had major consequences for the organization? Are there patterns? The purpose of this profiling is to see how well your organization has responded to external change (were you behind, abreast of, or ahead of these changes?) and to identify persistent blind spots. You may have been very well attuned to political changes, for instance, but repeatedly missed important technological developments.

Consider Royal Dutch/Shell, which has been justly praised for its pioneering work in scenario planning. Shell was better than its competitors in seeing major swings in oil prices in the 1970s, the overcapacity in the tanker industry in the 1980s, and various recessions in the Far East.[2] Yet Shell was badly burned by several external developments that may indicate a blind spot related to its public perception and the media. The first occurred in 1985 when the company, with the approval with the U.K. government, wanted to sink the Brent Spar, an obsolete oil platform, into the North Sea, hundreds of kilometers removed from any shore. While it may have been an effective engineering solution, Greenpeace made it a cause célèbre, resulting in European boycotts of Shell stations and a costly change in plans. Later that year, Shell got badly bruised in Africa because it had allegedly supported a military junta in Nigeria that was executing political opponents, and had also reneged on its promises to local communities.

While Shell was a very skilled engineering and oil company, these two episodes indicate that it was too rational or myopic in predicting societal responses to its action. Its planning teams tended to have more engineers than social scientists. To its credit, the company engaged in genuine soul searching about the deeper causes of the Brent Spar and Nigeria catastrophes, and it dramatically increased its attention to social and media issues by conducting systematic research of stakeholder concerns. It embarked on a major benchmarking project in this area and launched an impressive annual document reporting its work in corporate social responsibility. Several of these actions were pioneering in their own right. By identifying such persistent blind spots, companies such as Shell can direct more attention to examining overlooked parts of the periphery.

*Is there an instructive analogy from another industry?* Sometimes you can learn from the experiences of other industries. Find an analogous industry or market situation where companies have been blindsided from the periphery or have exploited an emerging opportunity. What lessons can you learn? Consider nanotechnology, which enables the creation of superstrong fibers, precision-guided smart drugs, and a host of other innovations by precisely manipulating materials at the molecular level. This emerging technology holds great promise—as did GMOs in Europe before activists fanned the fears of consumers and retailers began resisting. What can the developers of nanotechnology learn from the GMO debacle?

The potential social, legislative, and ethical issues raised by nanotechnology bear similarities to those that have bedeviled GMOs.[3] Preliminary toxicity studies, for example, have already raised alarm about the possible health hazards from nanoparticles. What's more, the potential use of nanotech-based sensors and tracers for food labeling raises privacy concerns. And nanotech developers are large global firms whose motives are often regarded with suspicion—a fact that could be exploited by activists trying to attract media attention and financing. Finally, there are no uniform rules governing the release and control of nanomaterials, which invites scrutiny and regulatory oversight.

None of these threats may materialize from the periphery, but it pays to be vigilant. Already there are early signs for concern. Reinsurer Swiss Re has cautioned against a rush into nanotechnology, citing its unknown risks.[4] One study reported brain damage to large-mouth bass swimming in an aquarium filled with nanoparticles

Opposition to GMOs took root in large part because the public could easily imagine GMO hazards but did not see clear benefits from modified seeds such as herbicide-resistant soybeans. It follows that, if the nanotech industry expects consumers to accept risks, it must also demonstrate tangible benefits. Are there analogies to the introduction of other controversial technologies, such as nuclear power, that might also be instructive for nanotechnology? Are there analogies to technologies that were more successful, such as the biotech and PC revolutions? Searching for suitable analogies can reveal unexplored risks and opportunities. What can be learned from them?

Searching for analogies allows managers to see their own situation through a different lens, helping to highlight important areas of the periphery that may be missed in current thinking. For example, Mitsubishi Chemical, one of the pioneers of nanotechnology manufacturing, particularly the carbon molecules known as fullerenes (or buckyballs), has embraced the lessons of the GMOs. Mitsubishi's Frontier Carbon company began laying the groundwork for the commercialization of fullerenes in 1993, a decade before its first commercial products were expected. It is actively addressing health and environmental concerns about the molecules. Recognizing that consumer concerns are heightened because there is no government-approved system for monitoring, testing, and certifying nanotechnology, Mitsubishi pushed for regulations. It worked with government, academic leaders, and other stakeholders to develop regulations to limit the exposure of people and animals to nanomaterials. Mitsubishi recognized that this preemptive collaboration and public trust are needed for the industry to succeed and avoid the post-launch public backlash that undermined GMOs; the experiences of GMOs highlighted the importance of addressing public opinion.[5]

*Who in your industry has a good track record in picking up weak signals and acting on them ahead of the competition?* In addition to studying negative impacts in your own company and industry, it is instructive to ask which companies have been especially effective in noticing changes on the periphery. What's their secret? In some instances, the remarkable insight may have been luck. But if an organization has repeatedly done a good job of seeing the periphery before others do, it may be worth emulating some of its underlying practice.

For example, the Branch Bank and Trust Company (BB&T) has been one of the fastest-growing banks in the U.S. South, with a footprint reaching from Florida to the Northeast. The company is skilled at identifying expansion opportunities, making 159 acquisitions of banks, thrifts, insurance companies, and other firms in a fifteen-year period. So, how do they do it? In this case, the leader sets the tone through the questions he asks and the actions that follow. BB&T is led by John Allison, who is recognized for his wide-ranging interests. Employees marvel at how he reads several new books each month, brings in speakers from outside the banking world, and encourages managers to explore. As chairman and CEO, he seeks to inculcate deep values, which include a sense of curiosity. These values help him and others spot new acquisition opportunities in banking as well as potential integration problems as new banks are add to BB&T. The company also uses a rigorous process to identify potential acquisition targets and screen them based on both objective criteria and more subjective factors such as cultural fit.

Each industry has its own success stories about organizations that scanned the periphery well. Making a list of such organizations, assessing their similarity to your own company, and exploring which best practices you might adopt is a good way to start improving your own peripheral vision. However, benchmarking against others is at best a starting point, a way to catch up and reduce your own vulnerability to surprises. To truly benefit from the periphery in a competitive sense will require more than dwelling on the past. You must also examine the present and future, as discussed next.

## Examining the Present

The next set of questions focuses on what you may be missing from your current environment. What are the signals that may be right in front of you that you are not seeing? How can you see them? What's happening in the areas where your attention is not directed?

*What important signals are you rationalizing away?* Almost all surprises have some antecedents, as Max Bazerman and Michael Watkins point out in their book *Predictable Surprises*, using 9/11 and Enron as prime examples.[6] However, people have a powerful tendency to ignore warning signals and pretend that all is well. The more intelligent we are, the better we also are at rationalizing away important signals of impending doom. By the time such weak signals emerge as a clear threat, it is often too late. For example, the assumption that falling foam insulation posed no serious threat to the space shuttle—an attitude the Columbia Accident Investigation Board called the "normalization of deviance"—unfortunately had catastrophic results.[7] The fundamental problem for managers here is to separate the signals from noise. It is not practical to assess each weak signal, and hence some seasoned experience is required to sort out the wheat from the chaff. While this may depend in large part on managerial intuition, careful reflection on which signals may be ignored can help to awaken this intuition.

To confront reality head on, managers should invite those in the organization, as well as those outside (such as channel partners, vendors, and industry mavens) to offer frank perspectives. The focus should be on signals or developments that are outside the organization's main area of focus and potentially threatening to the core.

But how do you identify important signals? A good way, we've found, is to select a signal and fast-forward its development using scenario planning (see figure 2-1) or other future-mapping techniques that stimulate managerial imagination. Another way to amplify signals and explore changes in the environment is to examine the world through specific lenses. For example, Cemex uses what it calls "innovation platforms" to think through creative options from shifts in its environment. One theme it considered was Regional Economic Development. Managers asked, "What opportunities are out there in regional economic development that we could exploit?" They then explored and identified two or three solid opportunities and moved to ideation, filtering, and development. As a result, the company recognized that it had to decrease the amount of time needed to provide housing to lower- and middle-income families. This realization led to an "accelerated construction" process.

FIGURE 2-1

**Cone of uncertainty**

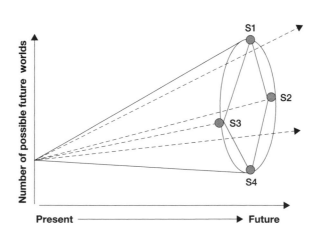

Note: S1 through S4 denote future scenarios.

Paying attention to insights from customers also can initiate this process. For example, a Cemex customer noted that a shortage of skilled labor was a critical challenge in building new homes. This led to the solution of providing molds that homeowners could use to make their own concrete blocks. Concrete could be poured into the molds just as in large factories, reducing the need for skilled workers. This became a business that produced close to $30 million in value for the company and reduced construction time for small homes from twenty-four to just three days.[8] By using a systematic process for thinking through the implications of changes or significant trends in its environment, Cemex was able to identify new opportunities.

*What are your mavericks and outliers trying to tell you?* Most organizations have mavericks with radical or divergent viewpoints on the periphery, but these insights are rarely tapped. Organizations also have connections with outside mavericks and other outliers or can cultivate such relationships. Your company must find informed individuals who eschew conventional wisdom and are thinking differently about the business. They may be mavericks who are congenitally unhappy with the direction of the business. They may be talented outliers in technology development or sales with insights into new customers and technologies that give them an idea for a new business. What shifting winds are they feeling that the rest of the organization is missing? As Andy Grove notes in his book *Only the Paranoid Survive*, most of these mavericks have a difficult time explaining their visceral feelings to top managers, who are usually the last to know.[9]

In addition to consulting with mavericks, listening carefully to the rank and file can help identify important insights form the periphery. Wisdom doesn't always flow from the top down, so listening for weak signals from within the organization is important, too. Effective leaders have wide internal as well as external networks. Some CEOs, for example, schedule periodic meetings with employees at multiple levels specifically to listen for weak signals.

Consider how drug maker Organon (part of Akzo Nobel) recognized the potential for a new antidepressant. The clinical trials for a new antihistamine developed by the company failed to prove its efficacy as a treatment for hay fever and other allergies. But a secretary involved in administering the trials noticed that some of the volunteers were particularly cheerful. This weak signal would have remained isolated at the periphery in many organizations. But when the secretary brought this insight to the attention of managers, thanks to a culture that encouraged dialogue, they explored the matter further. They realized that patients in the treatment group tended to be in better moods than those in the control group. Through chance and exploration, they discovered that this new drug was, in fact, an effective treatment for depression. Organon successfully developed and marketed the drug as Tolvon (mianserin hydrochloride). There are other examples of accidental discoveries in the pharmaceutical industry, from Fleming's penicillin to Pfizer's Viagra. (Interestingly, Fleming discovered the penicillin mold in 1928, but he didn't fully grasp its significance. It was not until 1938, when Oxford University pathologist Howard Florey happened upon Fleming's paper, that penicillin's true value was appreciated. And it was another three years before Florey's team completed human tests that revealed penicillin's astonishing therapeutic power. The weak signal Fleming picked up went unexploited for over a decade.) Only a vigilant organization can capitalize on such fortuity.

*What are peripheral customers and competitors really thinking?* Most managers rightly feel they have a good grip on the realities of their market, but they are usually focused on their current customer base and current rivals rather than on the broader pool of all potential customers and competitors. Naturally, companies must attend to the customers contributing the most to current earnings or to the competitors at the center of their radar screen. But companies can learn a lot from complainers and defectors, given that most companies experience between 12 and 18 percent "churn" or defections each year. Lost sales reports and postmortems on contracts won by competitors can be very revealing, but only if those doing the pathology are open to digging deeply and sharing their learning.

Companies can also learn about customer dissatisfaction by monitoring blogs, chat rooms, and Web sites (such as www.ihatemicrosoft .com) devoted to panning a product or company. By trolling Internet chat rooms, for instance, Procter & Gamble discovered unsubstantiated rumors in December 1998 that its fabric deodorizer Febreze was harmful to pets. The company responded immediately, gathering support from the American Society for the Prevention of Cruelty to Animals and other respected authorities to defuse the rumor and avert a large-scale consumer backlash.

Analyzing the "share of wallet" of your current customers (what percentage of a given customer's purchases in a category go to the company versus your rivals) offers a very different view than merely examining market share (how the total market is divided up). Where is most of the customer spending going? How can the company obtain a larger share? Listening to complainers and defectors and monitoring blogs (discussed in the next chapter) can offer important insights on these questions.

Companies can also consider a broader pool of customers. For example, Indian technology company ITC found a rich source of opportunity by shifting its focus from urban areas to rural villages (see box, "It Takes a Village").[10] What customers are you overlooking due to your current assumptions about the business? How could those assumptions be challenged?

Just as a narrow view of customers can limit opportunities, a myopic focus on direct rivals may obscure competitive threats from other directions. In industry after industry, from airlines and chemicals to mainframes, the long-term threats are more likely to come from those that offer cheaper rather than more sophisticated products or services. For example, the real competition for United Airlines proved

# It Takes a Village

While many companies focused their attention on accessible urban areas in India, ITC recognized the potential of peripheral markets in rural villages and found a way to draw them together through technology. According to conventional thinking, rural farmers are considered an unattractive market, with weak infrastructure, long distribution chains, and relatively low incomes. But ITC recognized the opportunity to use advanced communications technology to link rural farmers in India to global markets. It created electronic hubs, each sponsored by a local farmer, that served several surrounding villages.

These farmers, once dependent on local grain traders, could now check soybean futures on the Chicago Board of Trade through ITC's e-Choupal network, supported by PCs and satellite networks. The farmers also use the same system for e-commerce. These rural consumers were ignored by most companies, but by looking closely at this market and developing creative solutions to meet it, ITC created a thriving network.[a] By 2003, ITC had more than 3 million farmers connected through more than 5,000 hubs, handling $100 million in transactions. This was a significant opportunity in the hinterlands, far removed from the urban centers that had received the focal attention.

a. C. K. Prahalad, *The Fortune at the Bottom of the Pyramid* (Upper Saddle River, NJ: Wharton School Publishing, 2004), 69–72.

to be regional players such as Southwest Airlines rather than the other legacy airlines such as American Airlines. Incumbents should ask which low-end producers could enter their price-sensitive markets from the periphery. Similarly, managers should ask what threatening moves their partners might be making. Can they integrate forward or backward? None of Porter's five forces of competition can be safely ignored, especially nontraditional competitors with the potential to enter the market.[11]

## Envisioning New Futures

The past and present are good starting points, but they may not be the best indicators of what lies ahead. The next questions focus specifically on the future and so provide further guidance about how to effectively scan the periphery today.

*What future surprises could really hurt (or help) us?* Could there be future surprises or changes of the same magnitude as those that have already occurred? You may wish to project into your five- or ten-year view of the future the kind of volatility witnessed over the past four decades. For example, in financial services, what future surprises might be as big as the introduction of credit cards or the repeal of Glass-Steagall? If you are in a business related to home cooking, what future inventions could rival the impact of the introduction of the refrigerator or microwave?

Sometimes managers use an idealized future and then work backward to envision the surprises that must occur to realize this future. Russell Ackoff, the dean of systems thinking, calls this approach "idealized design" because the group is asked to design based on ideal point in the future.[12] For example, researchers at Bell Labs in the 1970s were asked to imagine that the entire Bell phone system had been destroyed. They were then challenged to envision and create the telephone of the future without worrying about present constraints or limitations. Unshackled from the past, the group envisioned such ideal features as voice mail, call forwarding, automated dialing, and voice commands. Although we are used to these features now, they were radically new functionalities at the time. They also far surpassed what AT&T knew how to deliver in the 1970s and inspired the development of new capabilities.

Similarly, W. Chan Kim and Renée Mauborgne's *Blue Ocean Strategy* invites managers to think beyond traditional industry and market definitions.[13] The real opportunities, they argue, are in the white spaces between markets, channels, and industries. They offer numerous examples of how firms managed to create new businesses in largely uncontested spaces. For example, Cirque du Soleil filled a gap between traditional circus performances and classical theater. They dropped the big-cost items (such as animals and star performers), added storyline and mystique, and used music in sophisticated ways akin to musicals. This hybrid offering became a runaway success without serious competition for many years.

Managers can also reveal weak signals by asking themselves how they would attack their own businesses as a new market entrant, either by setting up an internal team or bringing in outsiders. Recently, a team of consultants imagined a new-generation car company by challenging the car industry's conventional approach. In effect, it imagined a next-generation car maker that would sell mobility, not vehicles. They envisioned a "virtual" car maker that would outsource almost all activities, from design to logistics to leasing to service. Parts would be made by a network of suppliers in low-wage countries. Assembly would be done in micro-factories that would distribute low volumes of cars as close as possible to the local market. The company would lease the cars to customers and retain ownership for the life of the vehicles. Elements of this model—weak signals—already exist in a variety of industries.

*What emerging technologies could change the game?* Many companies are proficient at tracking developments in existing technologies that could affect their businesses, but this focus can deflect attention from emerging technologies that could be important in the future. For example, third-generation (3G) wireless communications technology was challenged by 2.5G performance improvements. This upgrade of the previous generation provided unexpectedly improved functionality that undermined the benefits of 3G.

Managers must focus their guiding questions on the customer conditions that might fertilize the emerging technology. Three groups of customers should be examined: those who are overserved, who consider the existing solutions more than they need; those who are underserved by these solutions; and those on the fringe who lack the skills and resources to benefit from the technology.[14] If the music industry had analyzed these customer conditions circa 1996, when the World Wide Web was emerging, it might have seen the peer-to-peer downloading phenomenon and realized that it met an underserved need: the desire for online access to a large catalog of unbundled tracks. With that understanding, legitimate file-sharing models might have emerged sooner and headed off the free-for-all of illegal file swapping ignited by Napster.

The choice of which technologies to track depends on the specific firm and industry, but there should be someone in the organization looking creatively at how new technologies could impact the business. This is what General Electric (GE) did with its destroyyourownbusiness.com initiative, in which business units were asked to apply Internet business models to undermine their current businesses. How far should managers go in looking at the fringes of technological developments? Most of the technologies that will affect the business in the short run—say, within a decade or so—are in a laboratory or journal somewhere right now, perhaps even in the company's own labs. The trick is for the leadership of the firm to be able to see the potential implications of these technologies before its rivals do. Similar explorations can be made of other trends such as demographic shifts, political changes, and other looming shifts in the environment.

*Is there an unthinkable scenario?* To see the full impact of potential future surprises, managers should develop at least one unthinkable scenario. This is a scenario that, while plausible, is considered so unlikely that it is dismissed as not worth considering. By explicitly entertaining these unthinkable possibilities—positive and negative—you can begin to recognize the many ways to interpret the signals in the current environment.[15] Without this intervention, the mind will naturally and forcibly fit any faint stirrings into pre-existing mental models. When subjects are shown a red spade in a deck of cards, for example, they often identify it as a heart because they force this anomalous card into the well-known model of the standard four suits; it is unthinkable that such a card might exist. But a viewer who has entertained the possibility of a red spade may be able to see it.

Because we are typically too certain of our own knowledge, we underestimate the true amount of uncertainty the future holds. For example, in the early 1990s, one of us was helping the Venezuelan oil company Petróleos de Venezuela SA (PDVSA) construct future scenarios. The usual unknowns, from oil prices to export markets, received much attention, but what actually transpired in Venezuela was *never* envisioned in any of the scenarios—the emergence of a populist leader, Hugo Chavez, who would challenge the establishment, declare martial law, nationalize the oil company, and fire all the top executives one Sunday afternoon during a national TV address, was an irrational scenario. Could signs of this possibility have been seen in the political landscape? Certainly they were there in retrospect, but this scenario was unthinkable, at least in the minds of those PDVSA leaders. Similarly, the fall of the Berlin Wall was an irrational scenario not envisioned by many politicians and organizations.

In contrast, when the federal credit union for Enron was developing scenarios in 1999, managers reluctantly considered the outrageous possibility that its corporate parent might collapse. At the time, this corporate juggernaut was praised around the world by investors, the press, and business gurus. But when this unthinkable scenario actually came to pass, the Enron Federal Credit Union was better able to react quickly and survive in part because it had entertained the possibility. Often the early warnings of pending turmoil are faintly visible at the periphery. Nonetheless, the credit union field has seen many cases where corporate sponsors suddenly vanished, usually due not to fraud but rather mergers and acquisitions, and the attached credit union often goes down with the mother ship. If you mine for these warning signs and then combine them into seemingly far-fetched scenarios, you may see the threats and opportunities at the periphery more clearly. Otherwise, you may simply dismiss or absorb the anomalies into your current worldview.

## Conclusion: Telescopes and Microscopes

At times the right scope will be a telescope to look out into the heavens. At times the right magnification will be a microscope to examine a small part of the world in great detail. If you are clear about the questions you should answer, then it becomes easier to establish the right scope to find answers. The questions in this chapter about the past, present, and future can help you illuminate areas of the periphery that might deserve more attention. You will see pieces of the puzzle that are missing and, like Sherlock Holmes, you can then pay attention to the fact that the dog didn't bark. Your scope can then expand to include these missing pieces so that, when you begin to connect the dots, you have the right dots to connect.

Our guiding questions are a robust departure point for a strategic dialogue about the scope of an active scan of the periphery. The choice of which questions to address depends on your strategy, previous pressure points in the environment, the concerns of senior management, and the weak signals being transmitted. The right questions will be further informed by methods for revealing uncertainties such as scenario analysis (demonstrated in chapter 5) and strategic risk management.[16]

The choice of scope—as revealed by the guiding questions—is not static. It is an ongoing iterative process for channeling the curiosity of the organization. (See appendix B for further discussion of search rules in economics and operations research.) You must continually review and refresh these questions, depending on the yield from scanning the current periphery. If a promising area reveals no information of interest, then perhaps you should narrow the scope. As the process for scanning and interpreting the periphery discussed in the following chapters yields new insights, these insights will also probably provoke new questions. This is truly a learning process for positioning your firm to anticipate what is coming around the corner.

Once the questions indicate a new area of the periphery to consider, the next challenge is how to scan in that particular area. For example, if your company recognizes its need to understand public opinion or look at unserved customers, how can it gather information about these unfamiliar territories? The next chapter considers the scanning process and offers a variety of approaches for scanning specific areas of the periphery.

# Chapter Three

# Scanning

## How to Look

*"It isn't that they can't see the solution.
It is that they can't see the problem."*

— *G. K. Chesterton*[1]

A MEDICAL DEVICE COMPANY challenged itself with a provocative question: "What emerging drug therapies could replace our device business?" With this question, the company expanded its scope, as discussed in the previous chapter, from looking at competing medical device makers to a much broader set of competitors and customers. Once the scope has been expanded, however, how can managers begin to answer such questions? To test its hypothesis, a team from the company was charged with creating a therapy or business model that could destroy its existing business.

This required team members to actively scan for new ways to think about the market, emerging technologies, and new business models. The question focused attention beyond traditional direct competitors in medical devices to potential rivals in drug therapies and relevant corporate and academic research. The team also needed to look beyond current customers and competitors, to scan consumer attitudes toward drug therapies in comparison with medical devices, and to consider the broader social and regulatory forces that could reshape the environment. To see more of the periphery, the organization had to change how it scanned.

The questions in the previous chapter help define *where* the organization might look for weak signals at the periphery. In this chapter, we consider *how* the organization can look in these new directions. To see new parts of the periphery, managers must use different scanning approaches. In this chapter, we offer a portfolio of scanning methods to capture and amplify the weak signals within targeted zones of the periphery: inside the firm; customers and channels; the competitive space (competitors and complementors); technologies, political, social, and economic forces; and influencers and shapers.

## Active Scanning

There is a difference between active and passive scanning. All managers scan, but they often do so passively. They keep their antennae up and wait to receive outside signals. They are continually exposed to a wealth of data ranging from the fuzzy impression of trade rumors to harder evidence from sales reports, trend studies, and technology forecasts. Managers monitor key performance indicators and other metrics for assessing accountability, maintaining control, and guiding Six Sigma initiatives.[2] (Although these systems may have constituted active scanning efforts when they were designed, most are now automated and passive.)

Although managers using this passive approach may feel in tune with the periphery, this may be a delusion. Because most of the data comes from familiar or traditional sources, this mode of scanning tends to reinforce, rather than challenge, prevailing beliefs. Because these metrics are tightly specified and focused on current operations, they are the antithesis of active scanning. There is no room for exploration. This passive stance narrows the scan and dulls the curiosity. Unexpected and unfamiliar weak signals will probably be lost.

Active scanning, in contrast, is often in response to a specific question, such as that asked by the medical device manufacturer or the guiding questions discussed in the previous chapter. Active scanning reflects intense curiosity and emphasizes the further-out and fuzzier edge of the periphery. For example, an advertising agency and its clients may passively scan results from television ad campaigns or trends in the industry. But managers could actively seek the answer to the question: "What are the consequences of more people surfing the Web and becoming increasingly skeptical of advertising?" Active scans often are hypothesis driven. If critical issues are involved, there should be multiple hypotheses.[3] Organizations entertaining multiple theories will more probably mount search parties using teams of outsiders and insiders, with diverse portfolios of methods. They use the scientific method of first proposing a hypothesis and then observing, speculating, and testing.

## Selecting Random Magazines: Directed Versus Undirected Scans

In directed scans, managers seek an answer to a specific question, but active scanning also can be undirected. Undirected scans involve more open exploration. For example, Buckminster Fuller developed a very personal and systematic approach to scanning the periphery. Whenever he was at an airport, he would randomly select a magazine from the stands in the bookstore and read it on his plane ride from cover to cover. On one trip the magazine might be about gardening, on another about fashion or airplane design. With each trip, Fuller learned something new and saw the world in a different way. Many managers could benefit from adding such vicarious reading discipline to their travel routines, especially now that we customize our computer screens and newsletters to report only what we deem relevant. Undirected searches may offer answers to questions that we do not even recognize or know how to formulate.

Active, open-ended scans are particularly important in turbulent environments where unexpected, outlying data might become more important. In complex environments, the scanning must be hypothesis driven but also open-minded. In stable environments passive scans might suffice, while in slowly changing environments a passive, open-ended approach could work. But, ideally, your organization uses both approaches as needed.

## Splatter Vision: Seeing the Forest and the Trees

Some combination of directed and undirected search may be ideal. The FBI, for example, trains its agents to use a scanning approach called "splatter vision." This involves scanning a crowd for would-be assassins by looking into the distance and not focusing on anyone in particular. Once the agent fixes a general gaze, he or she looks for deviation or change. Is someone restless, looking around too much, slowly putting a hand into a coat pocket? From among hundreds of faces, the agent seeks a lone assassin; suspicious activity then triggers a more intense focus.[4] By balancing directed and undirected scanning, a single agent can spot signs of trouble across a fairly large area.

When applying splatter vision to business, managers might use a broad hypothesis to help to focus attention, but they must also remain open to new information that might fall outside this original hypothesis. An organization might have a set of surveillance units broadly scanning the globe to answer strategic questions, combined with ad hoc task forces or mobile SWAT teams that can be directed to explore specific hot spots. This approach permits a wide scope of vision without requiring the cost and complexity of carefully monitoring every square foot of the globe in detail.

## Scanning Strategies for Specific Zones of the Periphery

Different areas of the periphery, as shown in figure 3-1, require different scanning approaches. Some are staples of competitive intelligence, technology forecasting, and market research. Others draw on new technologies for searching the Web or for achieving deeper insights into consumers through metaphor elicitation, lead-user analysis, trend tracking, and other approaches. We look at each of these areas of the periphery in turn and offer guidelines for practical approaches.

FIGURE 3-1

**Capturing weak signals from the periphery**

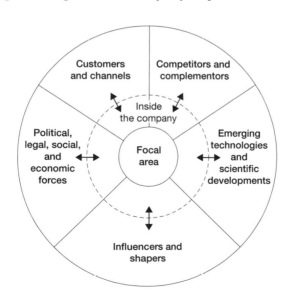

## Start Scanning Inside

The active scanning process can start with the insights locked inside the company. In many organizations, this internal knowledge is not well connected to decision makers. For example, a CEO at one company was collecting information about a tangential competitor. At a senior management team meeting, the VP for manufacturing casually mentioned that this same rival had been buying equipment similar to their own, a sign that it intended to compete head-on. This competitive intelligence was within the firm, but until this meeting the VP didn't understand the strategic issues well enough to know that it was valuable. The scale and scope of organizations create problems of uncoordinated, distributed intelligence. Literally, the organization doesn't know what it knows and cannot bring the collective insights to the surface and coalesce them meaningfully.

The larger the company, the more points of contact it will have with the periphery. Salespeople are in constant touch with customers, development teams hear gossip at trade shows, retail sales clerks register complaints and requests for new items, and finance people are aware of competitors' capital needs. Each point of contact has the potential to be a valuable listening post. For example, most companies have call centers, but many treat these call centers as costs to be minimized rather than as useful listening posts. Often, these contact people lack the expertise to recognize and interpret the weak signals appropriately.

To improve the ability to capture the peripheral insights within the organization, there must be (1) appropriate and visible channels for sharing information, (2) wide knowledge of the questions guiding the scan, and (3) incentives for actually sharing useful information. People must engage in frequent and free dialogue for the necessary connections to occur spontaneously. This, in turn, requires a culture of trust, respect, and curiosity, plus the recognition that information sharing is crucial. Too many companies still operate in a mode where information is shared on a "need-to-know" basis only. In chapter 7, we explore the capabilities for knowledge sharing in greater depth.

## Listen to the Voice of the Market

In addition to scanning inside, companies can look outward to customers or channels. Consumers may lead or change the intended use of a particular product in unanticipated ways, as with the use of cell phones for text messaging or Skin-So-Soft for bug repellent. While cell phone keypads were not designed for easy messaging, consumers (particularly teenagers) were so intent on messaging that they overcame design limitations through clever abbreviations. Consumers are also shaping the healthcare space by using vitamins and alternative approaches, such as chiropractic and homeopathic treatments, developed independently of mainstream Western medicine. The periphery of the market is often obscured, however, by the abundance of routine data from call reports, territorial sales data, news releases, periodic market surveys, and other sources.

The Internet has greatly added to the avalanche of signals, but it also creates opportunities to look into the thoughts of consumers to an unprecedented degree. Increasingly powerful tools can help monitor and interpret huge portions of the Internet, like satellite storm-tracking systems, to identify emerging patterns of business storms or sunny weather (see box, "Harnessing the Web").

The problem of seeing shifts in customers and channels is often hampered by arrogance ("We know what the market wants because we're out there selling to them") and complacency ("The information was good enough for my predecessors, so it's good enough for me"). Firms can overcome this insidious close-mindedness with a

# Harnessing the Web

What's the best place to find the next Madonna or other rising star in entertainment? One good place to look for advance signals in this area is by reading high school newspapers. Keeping up with U.S. high school newspapers is a daunting task in a print world, but electronic versions can now be scanned online and trends can be discovered from even these peripheral publications. By scanning the Web, a large corporation has the ability to tap into the thinking of an obscure teenage journalist.

While the Internet can create a dangerous data overload that could cloud peripheral vision, new technology can help extract insights. IBM's WebFountain gulps down huge quantities of Internet data to create a platform for active scanning and questioning. WebFountain ingests the Web at a rate of around 50 million new pages per day, including Web pages, blogs, bulletin boards, enterprise data, licensed content, newspapers, magazines, and trade journals, based on Web-access protocols and custom agreements with content producers. Most of the information on the Web is unstructured. WebFountain provides an integrated infrastructure for advanced text analytic solutions working with structured and unstructured data. The system is supported by ongoing IBM research projects—with more than 250 scientists in five countries working on advanced text analytic research.

WebFountain can be used to track corporate reputations and to detect negative publicity or investor discontent, track trends and competitive information, identify emerging competitive threats, and understand consumer attitudes. But the power of this tool will be no better than the quality of the questions posed by the user.

variety of methods for actively scanning the periphery.[5] Among the approaches are the following:

- *Monitor complainers and defectors.* Myopia about customers can be combated by learning from complainers and defectors, as discussed in the previous chapter. Both these groups of customers are expressing, albeit in rather different ways, a frustration that their needs are not being met. This can offer insights into the sources of growing dissatisfaction or into potential market opportunities (see box, "Mind the Blog").

- *Track the trends.* Keeping track of broader societal trends can help to identify opportunities to create new value. Consulting companies such as Iconoculture monitor trends about lifestyles and then examine how they create opportunities for business.[6] Other organizations track social trends (Yankelovich or Publicis), technology trends (Gartner or Forrester), or political trends.

- *Seek out latent needs.* The somewhat whimsical definition of *latent needs* as needs that are "evident but not yet obvious" contains a serious message. Seeking out latent needs addresses the shortcomings of structured market research methods that impose fixed scales to obtain standardized responses from large samples. While these methods capture differences in manifest needs that are close to the surface, they obscure latent needs and unsolved problems. Focusing on these latent needs is how Intuit learned how to move from personal finance software to easy-to-use versions of tax-preparation software and, later, to accounting software for very small businesses.

  Numerous techniques have been devised to help firms surface latent needs such as problem identification,

# Mind the Blog

On September 12, 2004, a bicycle enthusiast known only as "un-aesthetic" posted a note on an online discussion group revealing that Kryptonite locks could be picked with an ordinary Bic pen. The note was quickly picked up by prominent blogs and spread across cyberspace. A week later, the Kryptonite company, owned by Ingersoll-Rand, issued a noncommittal statement that its next line of locks would be "tougher." Dissatisfaction continued to spread, and the issue percolated from the blogs into the mainstream media, with stories in the *New York Times* and other publications. Driven by the media attention, an estimated 1.8 million people had seen the postings about Kryptonite by September 19. The

---

storytelling, and "laddering" methods to probe deeply for underlying beliefs.[7] Other methods, such as the observation of product purchases (as is done in the "antennae shops" of companies such as Sony and Sharp), in-depth studies of customer economics (including "spending a day in the life of a customer"), and metaphor elicitation, can further illuminate consumer values and attitudes. But all this deep digging will be of no avail without attentive listening to decode the messages in the stories and observed behavior.

- *Leverage lead users.* These are users who experience needs ahead of the market and are working to find a solution sooner. They even may have developed a novel solution already. Products such as correction fluid, sports bras, and Gatorade all owe their existence to lead users who were ahead of the broader market and started a mini-trend. Companies can learn from these lead users. For example, refrig-

company now had a serious problem. On September 22, just ten days after the original post, the company announced that it would exchange any affected lock for free, with an estimated price tag of $10 million.[a] As news anchor Dan Rather and U.S. Senator Trent Lott also have learned, blogs can move a weak signal from the periphery to the center very rapidly.[b] Companies can learn a great deal by monitoring them carefully. Some companies, such as Sun Microsystems, Google, and Yahoo!, have created their own blogs to actively communicate with customers and employees and to learn about emerging concerns at the periphery.[c]

a. David Kirkpatrick and Daniel Roth, "Why There Is No Escaping the Blog," *Fortune*, January 10, 2004, 44–50.
b. www.cnn.com/2004/TECH/internet/09/20/cbs.bloggers.reut/.
c. David Kirkpatrick "It's Hard to Manage If You Don't Blog," *Fortune*, October 4, 2004, 46.

erator makers might learn from scientists studying super-conductivity, which requires advanced refrigeration technology to achieve ultra-low temperatures.[8] Their needs for refrigeration may point the way to opportunities for innovations in high-end products for consumer or industrial markets (such as a flash freezer used by a fish wholesaler).

- *Seek instant feedback.* Customers can sometimes be involved in the product development process by participating in on-line communities. Prototyping software lets prospective customers create or modify designs, allowing companies to screen concepts instantly. Their reactions can also give early signals of potential problems. State Farm recently queried its new online community about the idea of discounts for safe drivers who had black boxes installed in their cars to monitor their driving behavior. Most of the panel didn't like the idea because they saw it as an invasion of privacy.[9] This small-scale test and quick feedback allowed the company to avoid the expense of a broader initiative.

- *Hunt for precursors.* Precursor analysis looks for a part of the country or globe where fads, fashions, or technology innovations tend to appear earlier. In the United States, California is often considered a bellwether state for social trends. Makers of toys, cell phones, video games, and cars are now looking to Japan for trends that will later appear in the United States and Europe. South Korea may offer insights into the future of broadband and wireless use in the United States and other parts of the world (see box, "Increasing Your Bandwidth").[10] Companies such as Converse use "cool hunters" and trend trackers as an early-warning radar to forecast emerging trends and market patterns.[11] Cool hunters roam the streets with cameras and notepads seeking emerging trends. Cool hunters have identified trends such as the rise of retro, which brought back Converse One Star sneakers, and the growing VIP culture, which is all about creating a perception of exclusivity through limited-edition merchandise, VIP rooms in clubs, and platinum cards.

- *Effectively mine the available data.* Retailers, banks, and the other organizations that collect mountains of data about their customers are using data-mining techniques to analyze their databases to extract patterns and trends. With new developments in predictive analytics, it is increasingly possible to forecast future trends. This use of data can help segment the market more effectively. An auto insurance firm learned, for example, that, while sports car drivers overall have more accidents, people who own a sports car as a second vehicle are no more accident-prone than other drivers.[12] Another valuable use of these techniques is to identify fast-growing market segments where the firm has just a modest presence.

# Increasing Your Bandwidth

What does the future hold for broadband and wireless? South Korea may have the answer. With broadband access to more than 75 percent of homes and cell phones in the hands of 75 percent of the population, Korea is a precursor that could point the way for other markets. Mobile phones have become a "remote control for life" as users tap into their bank accounts, check on sports, play games, and listen to music downloaded from the Internet. New phones that can read radio-frequency ID tags will tell users the expiration date of fresh produce in the supermarket. Smart homes in Korea have Internet-enabled refrigerators with flat-screen monitors and cameras to keep an eye on children after school. TiVo-like capabilities are ubiquitous, with fast and easy music and video downloads. Smart homes have wired Internet-enabled appliances, including air conditioners, microwave ovens, washing machines, and robot vacuums, all of which can be controlled remotely. On the drawing board are satellite-based broadband networks that can beam movies and television shows to cars in motion and smart toilets that can conduct tests and relay diagnostic information to family doctors daily.[a] As eBay chief executive Meg Whitman comments, Korea offers a "window into the possibilities" of high-speed broadband.[b] By looking at such precursors—and understanding the drivers of growth—you can increase your own bandwidth in understanding the potential implications of technological and market changes.

a. Peter Lewis, "Broadband Wonderland," *Fortune* (September 20, 2004), 191–198; "Korea's Broadband Revolution," *Chief Executive*, April 2004, www.chiefexecutive.net/depts/technology/197a.htm.
b. In "Man's Best Friend," *The Economist: Special Section—A Survey of Consumer Power* (April 2, 2005), 8.

- *Listen to channels.* Retailers, wholesalers, and other intermediaries are often the first to hear about changes with regard
  to end customers or new offerings from unheralded competitors. Of course, it may not always be in their interest to
  share what they know, but it is always worth a conversation.
  For larger suppliers and retailers, electronic connections can
  help monitor sales and trends. As economic value and
  power migrate downstream to these channels, it is even
  more important to see the market through their eyes and anticipate their moves. Where are they planning to grow? How
  many suppliers will they support? How quickly will they
  adopt radio-frequency ID tags to track products?

## Study the Competitive Space

For most companies, their rivals are squarely in their focal vision.[13] They are the topic of every strategic planning session, spe-
cialists are paid to watch them, and managers role play them in war
games to anticipate their moves and countermoves. An obsessive attention to a few target competitors is the key to survival in capital-
intensive industries where competition has been reduced to a zero-
sum game. Careful attention to signals from patent filings, lobbying
efforts, market tests, changes in hiring practices, and other moves of
direct rivals is laudable. How else can we understand the intentions
of our competitors? But if immediate and visible threats always take
precedence, management attention will be diverted from new competitors lurking at the periphery.

A laserlike focus on direct rivals not only leads to myopia but
also encourages imitative strategies and a demonstrable convergence
of incumbents on the same choice of value propositions and scope
of offerings.[14] When everyone starts to look and compete alike, uncontested spaces may open up that attract new entrants with different business models. The broader challenge, therefore, is to recognize rivals who are not competitors today but who could be

tomorrow. Among the antidotes to a myopic focus on direct rivals are the following:

- *Widen the angle of vision.* General Electric's erstwhile maxim that every one of its businesses be number one or two in its industry, while very effective in weeding out winners and losers, ultimately resulted in a keyhole view of the business. It led managers to define their markets narrowly to achieve the desired leadership position. This narrow definition limited the recognition of potential opportunities, and focus on a dominant share tended to dampen insight into creative new markets or approaches. So the company then asked the leaders of its businesses to reverse this frame—to define their markets in such a way that it gave them only a 10 percent market share. This shift meant that 90 percent of their focus was now outside their current business—on other competitors, regions, channels, and market opportunities in the periphery.

- *Watch out below.* Low-end competitors are often ignored or dismissed. Consider DuPont's experience in the 1990s. Early in the decade, DuPont managers began seeing a disturbing pattern of slowed growth across its businesses, ranging from old stalwarts such as Dacron polyester to newer businesses such as nylon engineering resins. As sales declined and competition intensified, large segments of the markets for these businesses were unwilling to pay a price premium for DuPont's superior products. Each of DuPont's businesses independently decided to focus on the more profitable high end of their markets, conceding the low-price markets to the new rivals emerging from the periphery. These low-end entrants parlayed increased volume into ever lower costs.

  The firm's widespread myopia about the significance of low-end competitors and its strategic retreats from markets led to sagging capacity utilization and increased unit costs, thereby exposing the company more to low-price competition. To learn from the past and better prepare for further attacks from below, a group of business managers got together to evaluate this new threat and the company's successful and unsuccessful responses. As they came to understand the threat and why so many business units were missing it, they developed processes for anticipating low-end competitive threats early and for developing preemptive strategies. This group of managers became the nucleus of an organization-wide learning network that went on to identify and eliminate the root causes of the company's blind spot.

Gary Hamel and C. K. Prahalad have observed that incumbents tend to dismiss competitors with meager resource endowments. They note that ". . . if there is one conclusion to be drawn from the endless shifting of competitive fortune it is this: starting resource positions are a very poor predictor of future industry leadership."[15]

- *Create a phantom competitor.* To sensitize the organization to a possible new player that could enter below the radar, assign a multidisciplinary team to create a phantom competitor that is ideally structured to succeed in the market. The team needs to draw on its knowledge of the points of vulnerability of the company and possible market shifts to spell out a full business strategy. The medical devices company mentioned at the beginning of this chapter did that, in effect, by assigning a team to examine how drug therapies might undermine its current business. Can the company itself adopt part of this strategy? Can the market situation be changed to reduce the chance that such a competitor could succeed?

- *Take cues from complementors.* Complementors can also offer insights into the potential intentions or early moves of rivals. A complementor is any product or service that increases the demand for your offering. For example, high-definition television (HDTV) required compatible programming before sales took off, and vice versa. Complementors may yield clues about the periphery and reveal the intentions of competitors. By looking at complementors, Sony discovered that Microsoft's Xbox was challenging the dominant share of the worldwide game console market held by PlayStation 2. Microsoft offered game developers a single platform of compatible programming tools to build games both for the Xbox and Windows-based personal computers. Because game software could run on both consoles, the advantage Sony gained from being the preferred platform for game developers might be jeopardized. By scanning the developers of the complementary software Sony recognized the threat posed by Microsoft's strategy.[16]

## See Where Technologies Are Going

A company's core technologies will obviously be its primary focus of attention, but what are the emerging technologies that might change the game? While agriculture may seem far removed from technological revolutions, farmers and farm equipment manufacturers must monitor advances in tractor technology (with new equipment guided by advanced global positioning satellite [GPS], for example), biosciences (with genetically engineered seeds), and online auction sites for selling grain and other farm goods. Many small farmers, in particular, were blindsided by these changes from periphery of their rural operations.

How can organizations keep an eye on such future possibilities while still tending the crops in the fields today? Among the approaches are the following:

- *Look in laboratories.* The prospects for many technological breakthroughs are often visible twenty or thirty years before they became an "overnight success." The computer mouse was first demonstrated in 1968, along with hypermedia and multiple windows, but it didn't appear on the market until 1989 as part of the Apple Macintosh.[17] The patent for facsimile transmission over wires was granted to Scottish mechanic Alexander Bain in 1843, but it did not become commercially viable, after many improvements, until the 1980s. Some future innovations may be in your company's own laboratories.

- *Scan broadly.* The exploration of potential technologies should be expansive. Attending a conference or spending a day reading through *Wired*, *Technology Review*, or *Scientific American* can be a low-cost way to survey the landscape. Academic and technical journals offer a deeper dive, although they require more time and expertise. In addition to the technology literature, there are many other places to scan for opportunities and threats from emerging technologies, including:

  1. Within the company by cross-divisional teams that promote cross-fertilization of discoveries

  2. Through public licensors of technology that offer searchable databases

  3. Infomediaries, such as Innocentive and Nine-Sigma, that connect companies that have problems with independent researchers who offer solutions

  4. Venture capital firms, which are adept at identifying emerging opportunities (many companies have created in-house venture capital funds for this purpose)

  5. Informal networks cultivated at scientific or trade meetings, which can offer insights on the convergence of work by independent researchers[18]

- *Look for convergence.* It may be very difficult to foresee the trajectory of a technology from the periphery because technological applications usually come through the convergence of streams of multiple technologies. The World Wide Web became a force when the parallel development of computer technology and online access came together. Cell phones took off with digitization. Voice over Internet Protocol (VoIP) systems emerged only after the increased penetration of broadband Internet.[19] Computer printing technology can be combined with advances in nanotechnology and micro-electro-mechanical-systems (MEMS)–enabled manufacturing at the submicron level to create new possibilities. A plausible result is desktop manufacturing, where plastic or metal parts are locally built, layer upon layer, according to directions from a computer. Further down the road, some see the possibility of making almost anything through advanced "printers" in garages that can transform carbon into virtually anything through nanotechnological manipulation based on computer instructions. To gain deeper insights into technology trajectories, look at the potential for convergence.

- *Think through the implications.* Once they identify potential technologies, managers must think about their implications. For example, an insurance company looking at genomics research might consider how the ability to map the genetic makeup of policyholders could transform its business based on actuarial models. An article in *Technology Review* on researcher Aubrey de Grey's work on extending life, potentially "forever," presents a life insurance company with even more complex challenges and opportunities.[20] Even if the extreme view of this theoretical work may appear to be a remote possibility, it raises the possibility of breakthroughs that could lead to significant shifts in longevity. Insurance companies, for example, are starting to offer longevity insurance to protect people against living beyond their assets. These policies guarantee a certain income level for life, akin to what a reverse mortgage might offer. Increases in life span would change the whole context for such offerings. How can life insurance companies write policies for clients who may live forever?

Organizations such as the Institute for the Future can help in understanding some of the broader implications of technology trajectories. The institute surveys a diverse group of experts to identify their views of potential future changes in the environment and then weaves these diverse insights on technological and demographic shifts into coherent technology maps. This analysis moves from an identification of the technology to an understanding of its deeper implications. Individual companies can explore what these broader insights mean for their specific markets and firms.

## Learn from Influencers and Shapers

Influencers and shapers are people, groups, and organizations with influence that is out of proportion to their size. Trade associations, analysts, media commentators, academic experts, think tanks, and consultants can help identify and shape trends. The insights and agendas of these groups can unite to explore possibilities at the periphery. Here are some of the more recognizable influencers and shapers:

- *Media.* Consider the damage from a poor rating in *Consumer Reports* or a negative report on business practices in the *Wall Street Journal* or *Financial Times*. The media can deeply affect a company, industry, or economy by helping shape the attitudes of customers, investors, and other stakeholders. As noted earlier, companies must increasingly monitor blogs, podcasts, and other forms of personal journalism.

- *Luminaries or mavens.* For specific industries, market mavens connect us with pertinent information and thus become central to word-of-mouth epidemics.[21] For example, a few researchers and clinicians may serve as gatekeepers on the flow of information about medical products. In financial services, respected analysts have tremendous influence on investment decisions. Ask yourself, What are these opinion leaders saying and what are the implications for the future of your business?

- *Cultural icons.* In sports, media, and entertainment, the opinions of a few can influence the thinking of many. From Bob Dylan to Madonna to Bono, these cultural icons often roam beyond their immediate domain to offer political and social advice. Map out which of these icons may affect your industry and markets. Many Hollywood stars have helped various environmental and social causes directly or through movies that they star in or produce (from *Free Willy* to *Schindler's List*).

- *Trade and tax policy negotiators.* Although these people are often out of sight, their ability to represent the interests of an industry in the negotiation of new trade agreements can change the prospects of the industry, for better or worse. The negotiations around China joining the World Trade Organization (WTO) and the creation of North American Free Trade Agreement (NAFTA) have had a significant impact on many industries. Which tax and policy changes could transform your business environment?

- *Lobbyists.* Every trade association and most large companies use lobbyists to scan the legislative and regulatory arena and alert their clients to critical events. Those with autonomy and a strong power base can have a huge influence on new policies. The negotiation of new Medicare drug benefits, for example, had tremendous implications for pharmaceutical companies in the United States, and lobbyists were actively involved in their design.

- *Legal and political leaders.* The corporate lawsuits filed by New York Attorney General Eliot Spitzer shook the financial services industry. High-profile prosecutions and new regulations such as Sarbanes-Oxley can have a tremendous impact on companies and their industries. By watching the leaders of such initiatives, you might see these changes coming. What legal and regulatory changes are being discussed or pursued that could transform your industry?

We should think of influencers as information aggregators and magnifiers. Their voices are respected, their opinions are often sought, and they are not shy about exercising their authority. They come in a wide variety of forms; and the way they exercise influence is highly dependent on the situation. But they cannot be ignored.

## Guidelines for Scanning

Many parts of the periphery may be important to scan. Once you have identified an area as important, you can then choose among approaches to investigate that zone. Leaders must manage the process of scanning to concentrate on important areas, pose the questions, and assemble the resources needed to actively scan. Leaders must also weigh the desire for a closer look at a specific area of the periphery against the resources needed for such a scan. A few general principles can guide this process:

- *Actively manage the process.* Active scanning begins with the guiding questions (from the previous chapter) that tell the organization which specific zones of the periphery it should look at most carefully. This can help to focus attention and resources on those areas of the periphery that are most important.

- *Use multiple methods.* The key to active scanning is to avoid overreliance on the methods and information sources that everyone else uses. To gain fresh insights, we must go beyond seeing what others see. Because each of the methods discussed in this chapter gives only partial and imperfect insights, it is important to use multiple methods. As we see in the next chapter, having multiple views on an issue also is crucial to good interpretation.

- *Weigh the investments.* After identifying potential fruitful areas for searching, the next step is to creatively generate a comprehensive inventory of possible information sources and methods that can feed the scanning process and then to rank each one's value in answering a guiding question. Value here is based on a ratio of the depth of possible insights to the cost of collecting the information.

- *Commit to scanning.* Once various active scanning methods have been chosen, there must be an organizational commitment to follow through. The pivotal questions will be, (1) How much should we budget for ongoing information collection? (2) Who will collect, collate, and feed information to the interpretation process? and (3) Who will review and act upon the results?

- *Treat scanning as an iterative process.* Scanning and scoping are intimately related. The results of your scanning may suggest a larger or lesser scope. Managers may recognize something of interest and then expand their scope or scan another area more closely. Each scan offers new insights that inform the next scan.

The meaning of any weak signal detected at the periphery will depend on the position and strategy of the company viewing it. For example, wearable computers, with chips printed on fabric, will mean something different for a fashion-oriented cell phone maker than for an ethical pharmaceutical maker. But both firms should start with a broad view of the possibilities for scanning and then focus on the most significant zones of the periphery.

This leads us to the next challenge of good peripheral vision. Once scope has been determined and signals have been identified from important parts of the periphery, managers must determine what these signals mean. Might the creation of a wearable cell phone in the lab lead to its widespread adoption? Could wearable medical devices woven into fabric disrupt the pharmaceutical firm, or will this innovation pass into obscurity? The diverse signals identified through scanning might fit together into many different coherent pictures. In the following chapter, we examine strategies for interpreting the fuzzy signals that are observed at the periphery.

Chapter Four

# Interpreting

## What the Data Mean

*"When people stumble onto the truth they usually pick themselves up and hurry about their business."*

— *Winston Churchill*

BRITISH EXPLORERS brought a tribal chief from deep in the mountains of an isolated Malaysian peninsula to the seaport of Singapore at the beginning of the last century. The goal was to determine what and how much this tribesman from the stone age would notice after a day of "sight-seeing" the ships, the tall buildings, market place and busy traffic of this thriving harbor city. At the end of the day, he recalled just one thing—a man carrying many bananas by himself in a cart.[1] This amazing spectacle was close enough to the tribal person's world of experience to be noticed and remembered. All the other images of Singapore that day had no meaning to him. He obviously could see the new buildings, ships, carriages, traffic, and oddly dressed people streaming by, but he lacked a frame of reference for these new images. These objects may have been at the center of his vision, but they were *peripheral* to the world he was accustomed to. He was unprepared to receive them. They went into his eyes and then got lost among the million of synapses in his mind. We may consider ourselves to be more sophisticated in our sense making than this tribesman, but we share a common human dilemma: we can see only what we are prepared to see. No matter how advanced and complete our scoping and scanning may be, we still must interpret what we are seeing.

The process of making sense is even more complex when it relates to peripheral vision. The images are, by definition, muddied and imprecise. They are distorted like the edges of a fish-eye lens, and there is a high noise-to-signal ratio. In human vision, the periphery lacks detail and color. The mind can easily jump to the wrong conclusions about something that is seen out of the "corner of one's eye." There is an old Native American story about a coyote that is pursued by a relentless predator. This hunter always seems to be just one step behind him and always to the side. It turns out to be a feather stuck to the side of the coyote's own head, which explains why no matter how fast he runs he cannot escape it. Many times, when it relates to the periphery, we jump to the wrong conclusions about what we are seeing. In other cases, we fail to understand a real threat or opportunity and don't see it until too late. Both of these mistakes are related to inherent weaknesses in our sense-making process as individuals and organizations (see box, "Filling In the Hole in Our Vision").

During the five months preceding the 9/11 terrorist attacks, the U.S. Federal Aviation Administration (FAA) received a total of 105 intelligence reports, in which Osama bin Laden or Al Qaeda were mentioned fifty-two times.[2] These reports, from the CIA, FBI, and

# Filling In the Hole in Our Vision

The human eye is missing a little chunk of its vision where the optic nerve attaches to the retina. But we rarely notice this missing piece of our perception because of the Photoshop-like program in our brain that fills in the hole seamlessly. Having two eyes helps fill in the empty spaces, but even looking with one eye, we do not see this hole. Similarly, we seal the gaps of our mental eye unconsciously and nearly automatically. Even though managers may recognize that their organizations have blind spots, they still may not know what they are missing.

U.S. State Department, were streaming into the senses of the government bureaucracy, but were not given the needed analysis to make them comprehensible. The FAA received reports from separate agencies that were not, by and large, communicating among themselves. Scanning was effective in collecting the information, but the crucial step of "connecting the dots" and drawing together the whole puzzle was missing. The full implications were not truly grasped until it was too late (see box, "Somebody Has Already Predicted It").

## A Picture Snapping into Place

Scoping and scanning (discussed in earlier chapters) are concerned with finding pieces of the puzzle, but how these puzzle pieces are put together matters greatly. Our analogy to a puzzle, however, simplifies the process. In most cases, the pieces fit together into a diverse number of possible pictures and once we snap into one view, it

## Somebody Has Already Predicted It

In many organizations, key insights may exist but often they remain unrecognized. In the 9/11 terrorist attacks, not only were key pieces of information not connected immediately before the attacks but a broader awareness of the potential for high-impact terrorist attacks was not acted on. The possibility for this type of attack had long been recognized. For example, Robert Kupperman, chief scientist of the U.S. Arms Control and Disarmament Agency wrote in October 1977, "a trained, quite small paramilitary force could take the City of New York—or other large metropolitan area—off-line for extended periods of time . . . If the obvious targets are examined, it is clear that terrorists need not resort to using nuclear bombs or biological agents to bring about devastation . . . Western nations, even the United States, are ill prepared to cope with any form of warfare other than conventional military response."[a] Another early report specifically painted the scenario of airplanes being flown into high-rise buildings by terrorists.

a. Robert Kupperman, *Facing Tomorrow's Terrorist Incident Today*, Washington, DC: Law Enforcement Assistance Administration (October 1977).

is very hard to change. Sometimes changing one small part of the picture can alter the entire picture.

For example, the ambiguous image in figure 4-1 can be transformed into vastly different pictures through the addition or deletion of a few features, as shown in figure 4-2. Human sense making is not typically a gradual process where a blurry picture slowly comes into view but rather a discrete process where the addition of a small piece of information can suddenly cause the overall picture

FIGURE 4-1

**What do you see?**

to snap into a different gestalt. This is why additional sources of information and diverse views can be so important in shaping the
overall picture. These additional perspectives might add small elements that could change the picture or enable an organization
locked onto the image of the mouse to also see the man.

Once this picture is locked, it is vastly more difficult to see other
possibilities. At the extreme, this leads to a phenomenon described
by cult researchers as "snapping." This occurs when a new convert
acquires a completely altered view of the world and everything is interpreted through this new and inflexible lens.[3] In less extreme
cases, we often accept a certain picture of the world, and this limits
our ability to see other views. While few organizations have the
power and prevalence of a cult in their employee's lives, there are organizational pressures to adopt a certain mind-set in most organizations. If everyone has agreed that the picture is a human face, it will
take a courageous individual to suggest that it can equally well be

**FIGURE 4-2**

**A man or a mouse?**

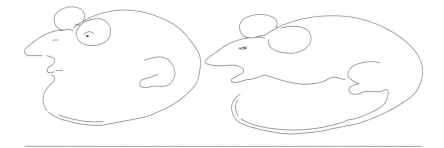

viewed as a mouse. There are a variety of individual and organizational biases that can hinder the accurate understanding of signals from the periphery, as discussed next.

## The Importance of Triangulation

Just as having two eyes allows humans to use triangulation and parallax for depth perception, the use of multiple perspectives in organizations can provide greater depth in peripheral vision (see box, "The Power of Parallax"). When General Motors (GM) developed OnStar, it could draw on its expertise in both technology and marketing to identify an emerging market opportunity. GM's success with OnStar is a well-known story of innovation, but the process by which this potential market was recognized and developed is less well appreciated. GM launched its OnStar service in its 1997 Cadillac line based on *telematics*, the integration of wireless communications, vehicle monitoring systems, and location devices. This new venture was about as far out on the periphery of the automobile market as can be imagined. First, OnStar had nothing to do with automobile design and production. Telematics had little to do with competition on price, reliability, or comfort, which had traditionally been the focus of competition in the industry. Finally, the market was miniscule. In the early days, OnStar President Chet Huber set a goal of bringing in fifty new customers a day in an organization that is used to counting its buyers by the millions.

How did GM manage to detect and act successfully on this peripheral opportunity? GM's acquisition of Hughes (and later EDS) gave it an early window on the technology of telematics. But the greatest unknown was not the technology but market adoption. In 1995, GM had commissioned a study of the key factors influencing consumers' decisions when purchasing an automobile. The study surfaced twenty-six factors, ranked according to importance to customers and current satisfaction.[4] GM found that, while customers

# The Power of Parallax

Parallax, which is a special case of triangulation, is the apparent shift of an object against a distant background due to a change in the observer's position. Because our two eyes are separated by just over two inches, people use the parallax of stereoscopic vision to see depth. Given the triangles formed by the two points of observation, the object, and the background, we can compute distances (either informally in our vision or more formally for astronomical or nautical calculations). To experiment, look at a nearby object against a distant background, closing one eye at a time. See how the object seems to shift positions horizontally? Similarly, in viewing the periphery, multiple perspectives (we are not limited to two eyes) can add to depth and detail, helping us to appreciate what we are seeing.

were very satisfied with how its products met their need for "mobility," four factors revealed important unmet consumer needs: (1) personal attention, (2) limited time and energy, (3) privacy, and (4) personal safety.[5] With these insights into the desire of customers for personal attention and safety, as well as an understanding of the emerging technology, GM managers recognized an opportunity at the intersection. By 2004, OnStar controlled 70 percent of the market with 2.5 million subscribers, generating an estimated $1 billion in revenue. Other firms were less astute in recognizing and acting on the potential of telematics. In 2002, for example, Ford Motor Company folded its joint venture with Qualcomm's Wingcast initiative, writing off a $100 million investment. While there are many reasons for OnStar's success, the triangulation of marketing insights and technology trends helped GM realize a big opportunity at the intersection.

Looking at the same phenomenon from different vantage points can achieve triangulation and help to identify where an object is in three-dimensional space. Unlike humans, organizations can draw on more than two eyes to comprehend what they are seeing. By bringing together all the "blind men" of the proverbial tale, they gain a more complete picture of the "elephant." Each single view may have its biases, but together they allow organizations to see what is really going on and identify new opportunities (see box, "An Entrepreneur Looks to the Skies"). This ability to gain a complete picture is particularly important in the periphery, where pieces of the puzzle may be blurry or missing entirely.

Our studies of best-practices companies such as Johnson & Johnson, Procter & Gamble, and IBM find that there is a deliberate attempt in such companies to obtain multiple perspectives to triangulate on the same guiding questions. This helps separate the weak but recurring signals of interest from the background noise. Multiple overlapping perspectives are crucial for the same reason we have two eyes. They permit us to triangulate and determine the depth of vision.[6] As Leonardo da Vinci observed, to truly understand any issue we must view it from at least three different perspectives.[7]

# An Entrepreneur Looks to the Skies

An entrepreneur trying to market a new driveway-coating business was spending $800 to send out advertisements to a general mailing list, with mediocre results. The former computer technician thought more broadly, recognizing a way to use a new online capability for satellite mapping available through Google Maps to identify neighborhoods with a high concentration of asphalt driveways. He then concentrated his marketing on these neighborhoods, resulting in a much higher rate of success and lower marketing cost. By looking beyond the confines of his own business and traditional approaches, he could see an application of a peripheral technology to his current business challenges.[a]

a. Kevin Post, "Satellite Photos Find the Market for Jet-Black," *The Press of Atlantic City*, July 8, 2005.

## Using Multiple Methods

No single method will suffice to see the whole picture because all methods are flawed or limited in some important respect. For example, managers seeking to understand an emerging technology might use analogies to markets for technologies with similar characteristics. But these analogies distort because the situations may not be comparable in critical but unknown respects. Surveys of experts using Delphi methods to assemble composite forecasts of future product demand may be no more than a pooling of collective ignorance. While any one method is limited, a combination of methods—each prone to different biases—deserves greater confidence.[8]

For example, instead of merely surveying potential customers, companies can sometimes get a better sense of the demand for a new technology by using different approaches. In the early 1970s, Xerox estimated the potential demand for fax machines by analyzing the extent and frequency of urgent written messages. It then contrasted the capability of fax machines to existing solutions such as mail, telephones, or telegrams. Using this approach, the company foresaw a business market of approximately 1 million units in the early 1970s, a number that proved too low in hindsight but was much larger than other methods predicted. (Xerox, however, bet on the wrong technology to meet this need, computer-to-computer transfers rather than specialty devices, and so missed capitalizing on its powerful insight.)

## Using Scenarios to See Both the Man and the Mouse

In addition to identifying diverse perspectives and approaches to any given challenge, scenario planning offers another way to look at an issue from multiple angles to decode a set of signals from the periphery. For example, a major newspaper company used scenario planning to look at a single technological innovation from several different perspectives. It could then examine a given new signal through the lens of each scenario. For example, the newspaper industry heard in 1999 that Xerox had introduced a new service to deliver customized newspapers electronically to hotels and other locations, allowing users to print out tailor-made content. Travelers to foreign places, for example, could get their local news delivered or read the leading national newspaper in their native language.

How important was this signal? Would it mean that hotel guests would never again hear the familiar thump of a newspaper outside their doors, or would it be a nonstarter? The answer depends on the scenario. In a scenario of "business as usual," this new service represents a niche market (the traveler's market) and a welcome alternative channel of distribution in addition to the physical delivery of newspapers. It might create new opportunities for newspapers to move beyond their natural geographic area as well as enhance customer loyalty. In another scenario, called "cybermedia," in which electronic channels are adopted rapidly, this initial foray into customized printing in hotels may herald the customized home printing of newspapers. Such a development could undermine the very asset base that newspapers depend on today (their printing presses and physical distribution network) while finer segmentation of the market could erode traditional advertising. In this world, newspaper presses, delivery trucks, or broadband mass-advertising messages are no longer needed or valued.

By looking at this single weak signal through multiple lenses, the managers could better explore its potential implications. If they assumed that the world remains "business as usual," they might undervalue this signal. On the other hand, if they assumed that the world would definitely be a "cybermedia" world, they might overreact. While such scenario-based analyses don't eliminate the uncertainty about either the development of the technology or consumer acceptance, it can help managers understand more when one small piece of the puzzle is added. They can now see more possibilities than just the familiar "bananas" from years past.

## Seeing Both Customers and Competitors

Companies also can suffer from focusing too narrowly on either customers or competitors rather than looking at both. When Eckhard Pfeiffer became CEO of Compaq Computers in 1991, he recognized that the company was focusing primarily on competition with IBM but was overlooking the shifting demands of customers as a result. This obsession with IBM meant that Compaq wasn't willing to engage in second-tier pricing to reach a broader consumer market and consequently had lost market share to low-priced competitors. If it had focused more on customers rather than tracking its progress against IBM, Compaq might have more quickly recognized the important shifts taking place in the market for personal computers. On the other hand, a magazine publisher that focuses only on customers will stay in tune with the needs of the market but fail to see the potential consolidation of rivals or shifts in technology that could bring new players into the market. Companies must look at competitors *and* customers (as well as other stakeholders) simultaneously. An exclusive focus on one or the other creates significant blind spots.

By looking closely at its customers *and* competitors, a company that owned a major carpet-manufacturing business forced its management team to face up to three unpleasant realities: its fiber suppliers were growing in power because of the visibility of their brands with end consumers, its retailers were consolidating and wielding more power, and the manufacturer did not have a differentiated product. With this recognition, the company exited the carpet business. By surfacing and challenging its mental models, the managers could recognize these threats on its periphery. Eventually, they realized that they no longer had a viable business.

These are just a few examples of how multiple perspectives and methods can aid in the interpretation of signals from the periphery. Overlaps in scanning on the same issue may appear inefficient, just as having two eyes may at first appear to be a redundancy in human vision. But these overlaps serve an important purpose. They permit a cross-check against one another and so can be used to verify a weak signal. And they help to compensate for deficiencies in our individual and collective vision, as discussed next.

## Why We Are Blindsided

Why do we struggle to grasp what is at the periphery? Our ability to see is limited by our mental models and other perceptual distortions (see box, "Sight Versus Seeing"). We can offset our various individual cognitive and affective biases partially through multiple viewpoints.[9] We must respect and guard against these biases. Yet even

# Sight Versus Seeing

There is a difference between taking in a signal and actually seeing what is happening. Scientists believe that images a baby sees during the first few days of life are upside down and that they are ultimately inverted through the child's contact with the world. We appear to retain this flexibility into adulthood. In one fascinating psychological study, subjects were asked to wear inverting lenses that flipped the images they saw. At first the participants saw everything upside down, as we would expect, but after a few days the subjects reported that the images were right-side up. When they took the glasses off, their normal vision was upside down (for a while).[a] There are also disorders where the visual portion of the brain is damaged such that patients can see a physical object but not recognize it. For example, they can copy a picture of a bird perfectly but identify it as a tree stump.[b] And there is the well-known case described by Oliver Sacks where a man with functioning vision mistook his wife for a hat. Clearly there is a difference between sight and seeing. As Immanuel Kant emphasized, there can be no perceptions without *preception* (the mental categories we use to organize reality in our minds).[c] For example, we cannot see a bird or fish without first having the precept or concept of such animals in our minds. We often see what we are looking for. This is why the tribesman was prepared to see only the cart of bananas on his trip to Singapore.

a. www.physlink.com/Education/AskExperts/ae353.cfm.
b. Steven Pinker, *How the Mind Works* (New York: Norton, 1997), 19.
c. Immanuel Kant, *The Critique of Pure Reason* (London: Macmillan, 1933).

when these multiple views are present, organizational biases such as groupthink may shade the periphery, even in organizations with a broadly defined scope and active scanning.

What we can see is greatly shaped and delimited by our mental models. These models are often tacit, functioning below the level of consciousness, and thus cannot be easily analyzed or challenged. Once we accept a certain model, we often force-fit reality into it (see box, "Missed Signals at Pearl Harbor"). For example, an R&D manager in consumer appliances may work from a model that says product design is a low-level cosmetic function to be done at the last minute. Managers at companies such as Braun, on the other hand, recognize

---

# Missed Signals in Pearl Harbor

On the morning of December 7, 1941, the captain of the destroyer *USS Ward* heard the sound of muffled explosions coming from Pearl Harbor on the mainland. Earlier, this captain had dropped depth charges on an enemy submarine moving into the harbor, just before it could surface, and had apparently sunk it. Yet when the captain heard the muffled explosions while sailing back to port, he turned to his lieutenant commander and said, "I guess they are blasting the new road from Pearl Harbor to Honolulu." Despite his unusual encounter with a foreign submarine that morning, he made sense of the exploding sound using his peacetime mind-set and failed to notice the signs of the first hostilities between the United States and Japan. His peacetime mind-set was so dominant that he forced the sounds of explosions into a road construction context rather than recognizing that air attacks were actually taking place.[a]

a. This example was offered by Sidney Winter, adapted from Roberta Wohlstetter, *Pearl Harbor: Warning and Decisions* (Stanford, CA: Stanford University Press, 1962); and Gordon Prang, *At Dawn We Slept* (New York: Penguin Books, 1981).

that good design not only appeals to the eye but should also be reliable and economic to manufacture and service. They consider product design at the start of the process of new product development.

A variety of cognitive and motivational biases seems to conspire when humans try to form a balanced judgment about a complex situation, such as an ambiguous signal from the periphery (see box, "Biased Interpretations"). Whenever multiple pieces of evidence point in opposite directions or crucial information is missing, the mind starts to twist and turn the facts to fit our preconceptions. The knowledge gaps are filled with tacit assumptions or inferences that often bias the opinion in a predetermined direction. This subtle process happens in largely unconscious ways and explains why people can hold such totally opposite views about issues, even when they are based on common and shared information. From jury verdicts to opinions about the Iraqi war, or such contentious topics as abortion or capital punishment, opinions are held strongly and new evidence is often filtered to confirm prior beliefs.

## Organizational Biases

In addition to personal biases, individuals in an organization often suffer from what Irving Janis terms *groupthink*.[10] They begin to think, act, and even dress alike. For example, General Motors ultimately took the Corvair off the market because of serious safety problems, many of which were already known but initially downplayed internally. As J. Patrick Wright writes in *On a Clear Day You Can See General Motors*, none of the top managers in GM "would purposely build a car that he knew would hurt people." Yet the internal push to meet sales and profit numbers led them to overlook "serious doubts that were raised about its safety" and then to "squelch information which might prove the car's deficiencies."[11] Only after consumer advocate Ralph Nader publicly pointed out the car's engine failures and safety problems in his 1965 book *Unsafe at Any Speed* did GM pull the Corvair from the market.

# Biased Interpretations

Although true objectivity may remain an elusive goal, managers must be aware of well-recognized traps underlying human inference and judgment. We describe the major ones here, with brief examples, in terms of how information is filtered, interpreted, and often bolstered by our seeking additional information aimed at confirming our prior leanings. The net effect of these biases is that we frame a particular issue in a certain way (without fully appreciating other possible perspectives) and become overconfident about our view.[a]

- **Filtering:** What we actually pay attention to is very much determined by what we expect to see. Psychologists call this *selective perception*. If something doesn't fit, we often distort reality to fit our mental model rather than challenge our assumptions. A related phenomenon is called *priming*. If we are about to be shown an ambiguous figure (such as the mouse or man earlier in this chapter), we may be predisposed to see interpretation A over B if an hour before or so we have seen interpretation A in a different context. For example, if we have read a line from a poem that made reference to a mouse, our chances of seeing a mouse in that earlier figure would go up. Last, there is an important motivational bias we must guard against, namely *suppression*, or the refusal to see reality for what it is. The extreme example is that of the mythical ostrich burying its head in the sand on seeing danger and hoping the threat will thereby disappear.

- **Biased inference:** Whatever information passes our cognitive and emotional filters may be subject to further distortion. One well-known bias is *rationalization*, interpreting evidence in a way that sustains a desired belief. We fall victim to this, for example, when trying to blame our own mistake on someone else or on external circumstances. Often this process works unconsciously because we are trying to reduce the cognitive dissonance between our knowing that we are wrong and the positive self-image of ourselves as people who do not err often. *Wishful thinking* is a related motivational process in which we see the world in a pleasing way. We see the glass as half full rather than half empty, or we deny the subtle evidence that a child is abusing drugs or that a spouse is cheating. Another common interpretation bias is *egocentrism*, the tendency to overemphasize our own role in the events we seek to explain. This self-serving tendency relates to the *fundamental attribution* bias, according to which we ascribe more importance to our own actions than to those of the environment. In other words, we view ourselves or our organization as more central in the overall system than it really is.

- **Bolstering:** Not only do we heavily filter limited information and often subject it to slanted interpretations, we may then bolster our case by searching for additional evidence that further confirms our view. For example, we may disproportionately talk to people who agree with us or actively seek new evidence that confirms our perspective, called *confirmation bias*, rather than pursuing a more balanced search strategy that includes disconfirming evidence. So, over time, our opinions may freeze and our attitudes harden as we immunize ourselves against contradiction. Indeed, we may even engage in *selective memory*, conveniently forgetting those inconvenient facts that don't fit the overall picture. The *hindsight bias* similarly distorts our memories so that our original doubts are erased. Thus, a vicious circle is created in which we exacerbate the earlier biases and trap ourselves in a self-sealing cocoon of half truths.

This depiction presents an extreme case (like a perfect storm) in which all errors point in the same direction. Fortunately, human beings do have considerable capacity for critical thought and do recognize that their views may be slanted and self-serving. But few appreciate the scope and magnitude of these biases or the fact they often conspire to hide the truth from us. Inquisitive managers and organizations must recognize that critical inquiry requires having an open mind, testing multiple hypotheses, and listening to the data to learn what it is really saying. Especially at the periphery, the risks of self-delusion, sloppy thinking, and jumping to false conclusions can be very large and very dangerous.

a. J. E. Russo and P. J. H. Schoemaker, *Winning Decisions* (New York: Doubleday, 2002).

---

Similar problems of groupthink surfaced in the *Challenger* disaster. How do managers who are generally deemed good and smart people make such bad decisions? Research shows that two heads are not necessarily better than one. Groups are better than individuals at seeing and responding to stimuli *only* if they have effective processes. The true relevance of various snippets of information can only be appreciated when they are shared and merged into a larger mosaic. Information sharing matters especially at the periphery because it overcomes the problem of distributed perception and memory when shared across organizational boundaries. To avoid information overload, however, managers must align vision and strategy so every member of the group can see the bigger picture and knows how his or her perspective fits into it.

Sense making occurs in a complex social environment where people are not just sensitive to what is being said but also who says it. In essence, we judge both the signal and the source as we assess the meaning of information. Source credibility is influenced by many factors such as status, past experience, and politics. Because most managers receive information from multiple sources, they must watch for possible biases. For example, when a doctor sees a new patient complaining of flulike symptoms, the physician already has in mind a relative rank order of various hypotheses that could explain the symptoms.[12] However, we often rely on educated guesses or hunches instead, and this is where various biases may creep in. For example, the doctor may not trust the patient to give reliable answers and therefore may discount a weak signal. Or the opinions of fellow physicians may be weighted not just according to their expertise but also in terms of their social standing and power status. Sociologists have conducted many studies on how the social networks in society affect the flow of information, from interlocking boards in the corporate world to the adoption of a new product in a local neighborhood.[13] These sociological biases are especially significant when the information is weak or incomplete, which is usually the case when dealing with the periphery.

Individual biases highlight why you must combine different perspectives on the same issue. The organizational and group biases, however, show that the way these different perspectives are cultivated and connected affects the ability of the organization to comprehend the surrounding world.

## Improving Sense Making

How can individuals and organizations overcome their inherent biases and blind spots to improve their sense making? Here are a variety of approaches that can help.

- *Seek new information to confront reality.* Larry Bossidy and Ram Charan discuss how the data-storage company EMC missed key changes in its environment that caused a rapid

decline in sales in 2001. EMC's sales force, speaking with
CIOs, was confident that orders were simply being delayed;
it interpreted the downturn as a temporary blip. But when
Joe Tucci was named CEO in early 2001, he began speaking
to CEOs and CFOs at customer firms and found that they
were changing how they did business. They were not interested in paying a premium for top performance, and they
wanted software that could link to the devices of other manufacturers. IBM and Hitachi were selling machines comparable to EMC's at a lower price. As EMC's market share
slipped, Tucci rapidly transformed EMC's business model
to focus more on software and services than on hardware,
which was becoming commoditized. Once Tucci recognized
the new reality, the company could transform its organization and respond appropriately. As Bossidy and Charan
note, the greatest business failures are often not due to
poor management but rather to the failure "to confront
reality."[14]

- *Formulate multiple hypotheses.* Organizations must develop
  competing hypotheses about the world rather than pursuing
  the simple single answers. For example, the physicist
  Michael Faraday accidentally discovered induction current
  when he noticed that his voltmeter moved after he changed
  a magnetic field around a wire. Many other physicists might
  have seen this brief change in the dial but did not realize its
  profound scientific significance. But Faraday was deeply
  knowledgeable and interested in magnetic fields. He had an
  open mind and was truly creative, entertaining multiple hypotheses. Organizations must, likewise, develop multiple
  hypotheses about the meaning of weak signals. Unfortunately, organizational sense making is usually driven toward
  one single meaning, so new data are force-fit into the exist-

ing mental model.[15] Managers may have limited tolerance for ambiguity and be reluctant to devote additional time to develop alternative hypotheses.

- *Encourage constructive conflict.* The lure of conformity and the power of groupthink tends to limit conflict. Conflict can, however, be constructive, especially when it is focused on tasks rather than relationships or personalities. A number of studies confirm that moderate conflict over tasks leads to superior decisions. This moderate conflict can push team members to create a more robust frame, gather better intelligence, explore more options, and examine issues in more depth. It allows the peripheral vision of individuals on the team to be considered in the group process. In contrast, more harmonious teams will probably miss key pieces of the puzzle. Crucial information may be sitting right at the table, but remain locked in the silent minds of individual team members who don't speak their mind because of subtle but strong pressure to agree.

  While close-knit groups can lead to dysfunctional groupthink, less rigid groups can often outperform the individuals in the team. James Surowiecki, in *The Wisdom of Crowds*, contends that in many instances groups can make far better decisions than individuals.[16] This is particularly true when companies create mechanisms (such as Delphi polling) to pool the collective wisdom of the organization without fostering conformity. Creating anonymous opinion markets is one way to avoid collective myopia. For example, in the 1990s, Hewlett-Packard asked employees to participate in a newly created opinion market to forecast its sales. Employees would bet in this market at lunch and in the evenings, showing through their investments their view of where the market was headed. This market's forecast beat the traditional company forecasts 75 percent of the time. More recently, a division of Eli Lilly asked employees to assess whether drug candidates would be approved by the U.S. Food and Drug Administration (FDA) based on profiles and experimental data, and the internal company market correctly identified the winners from a set of six candidates.

- *Tap localized intelligence.* Michael Mavaddat, one of the founders of the technology firm Intelligent Pixels, based in part on research on insect vision, notes that insect vision is very different from human vision. "Insects use a compound lens system, where most of the acts of seeing and noticing take place in the eye itself as opposed to the brain," he says. "Insects have phenomenal peripheral vision, not only due to their compound eye structure but also due to the 'localized intelligence' at the level of each eyelet. They sense a change in the periphery when adjacent eyelets compare results with each other and draw the conclusion that the world is changed."[17] For example, bees flying through a tunnel maintain equidistance to the side walls by balancing the apparent speeds of the images of the walls. In contrast to more centralized sense making, sometimes organizations must derive more of their intelligence and sense making from local levels in the organization. Terrorist networks have demonstrated the deadly power and resiliency of such an approach, using nearly autonomous cells that see and think locally. More positively, Linux and the open-source movement have used local design to build an ongoing global software project.

- *Use dialogue to share the big picture.* Individuals in the organization must see where the information might fit into the bigger picture. Otherwise, this disconnected information will sit idle. People must engage in frequent and open dialogue.

Too many companies still share information on a "need-to-know" basis only.

One way to achieve these seemingly conflicting objectives of organizational convergence and divergence is to create multiple scenarios for the future, as discussed earlier. Each scenario should paint an internally consistent story about a future that might emerge. By considering multiple scenarios at the same time, the organization can keep from being locked into one view of the future while sharing a common set of frameworks for discussing new signals.[18]

Where organizations normally filter out weak signals from the periphery, especially those that don't fit the dominant world view, scenario planning systematizes the hunt for weak signals that may foreshadow fundamental shifts in the market place and society at large. Rather than muffling weak signals, scenarios can magnify "postcards from the edge" so that they are visible to many more eyes. Because multiple scenarios are presented, in which a particular weak signal may have varying degrees of strategic significance, the organization avoids the trap of being overconfident and locking into one single view. Scenarios preserve the uncertainty that is inherent when studying the edges of the world.[19]

## Conclusion

We have examined the challenges humans and organizations face when making sense of ambiguous information and how we might address these challenges. At the individual level, the major problem is that humans fall victim to various cognitive and emotional biases without being very aware of them. Although these biases afflict all kinds of human judgments, they have freer rein when more ambiguity is present, such as at the periphery. When the data are clear and convincing, it is easier to engage in proper sense making. But when ambiguity is high, we can easily torture the weak data until they confess to whatever we want to hear or see.

Better information sharing and triangulation can help overcome these biases of interpretation. But in addition to doing a better job of "connecting the dots," managers can also gather more information to better understand what is happening at the periphery. This process of probing and learning about the periphery is the focus of the next chapter.

# Chapter Five

# Probing

## How to Explore More Closely

*"A thinker sees his own actions as experiments and
questions—as attempts to find out something. Success
and failure are for him answers above all."*

— *Friedrich Nietzsche*

AFTER BRINGING an eighteen-foot handmade canoe, golf
clubs, and Harley-Davidson motorcycles into memorial
services, it was clear to John Carmon that attitudes toward funerals
were changing. He was seeing a shift in mind-set from mourning
death to celebrating the life of the deceased (on the model of the Irish
wake). "There is major change in the way that people view their
ties to spirituality," said Carmon, president of Carmon Community
Funeral Homes in Connecticut. "Years ago, when death occurred,

people would reach to their religious traditions. Today, it is more about the person and where they fit into the larger scheme of things. It is much more personalized."[1]

In the United States, a decline in participation in organized religion as well as a passion for personalization had led to shifts in attitudes toward death and memorial services. There is an increase in cremation, which allows for more flexibility in the timing and nature of services than does traditional burial. This increased use of cremation reflects not only changing attitudes but also a more transient society and the shortage of cemetery space in some metropolitan areas.

Given these early signs of change, how might Carmon and other funeral home owners learn more about these changing attitudes and what they portend for their business? In response to the wishes of families, Carmon had experimented with more individualized services; now he was prepared to launch a broader experiment. In April 2005, Carmon opened a new Family Life Center in Avon, Connecticut. It looks nothing like a traditional funeral parlor. The center is designed for flexibility and nontraditional services. Wired with a fifty-inch flat-screen television to display photos and videos during the service, the center offers Web-streaming Internet technology so that remote participants can watch and send e-mail comments in real time from anywhere in the world. Carmon has even added a part-time events planner to his staff to help provide the kind of attention to detail that people typically reserve for weddings or other major life events.

While most funeral homes serve a very small geographic area, the new center is expected to draw people from a broader region in the way that wedding reception halls have done. But this initiative entails many assumptions and is yet to be fully tested. While it is an unproven model, Carmon and his team have worked hard to shape and sharpen their hypotheses. In addition to looking closely at market trends, they have analyzed demographics and conducted a community survey in the area where the new center is located; it seems like a market where this Family Life Center might work. Still, the true test is opening the doors. "This is taking a big chance in a brand new market," Carmon said just before the opening of the new facility.

In its first two months of operation, the new facility served eleven families and the reaction was overwhelmingly positive, particularly to the new technology such as Web streaming. In fact, the significance of this to one family in Florida led to a front-page article in the *Hartford Courant* that was picked up in four other metro markets around the United States and led to a follow up interview by CNN. Carmon notes that "The true test will be after a year of use and continued acceptance." But already he is rolling out plans to expand the approach to his other locations, with plans to add Web cameras in two more locations over the next two years, along with projectors, screens, and DVDs for picture tributes.

## Act Without Overreacting

When a business leader such as Carmon notices that families are asking to bring canoes and motorcycles into services or that rates of cremation are rising, how should he respond? Will these trends continue? How can the organization better understand the implications of these changes? The first step, very often, is to probe the periphery. This allows the organization to turn its attention to various weak signals and look more closely at them. As we have discussed, signals at the periphery are usually blurry and without color. Once an interesting set of signals has been identified, the challenge becomes when and how to add detail by looking more closely.

The key, however, is not to overreact. After all, the signals are weak and blurry. They could mean anything, and there is still great uncertainty about what these tea leaves foretell, if anything at all. Will the trend toward celebrating life continue, or will there be a backlash and return to tradition? Will the trend accelerate or take unexpected turns? Will the funeral business move in entirely new directions? While cremation has grown rapidly, new eco-friendly burial sites have been created, offering windswept fields and natural burials instead of traditional manicured lawns. In these woodland cemeteries, the dead are buried without embalming in biodegradable coffins.[2] Will this trend spread, eroding the interest in cremation? What impact will it have on the industry?

Probing strategies are designed to gather more information, to conduct experiments and develop options, and to better understand what the peripheral signals are all about. Sometimes this means looking more broadly for information to test a hypothesis. Sometimes it means designing an experiment, as Carmon did. And sometimes the signals are about nothing and should be ignored.

Carmon operates a portfolio of eight funeral homes, most of which are very traditional. He didn't move his entire business to this new model. He views the new Family Life Center as an outpost and a learning opportunity. Approaches that work well there will shape the company's offerings in other communities in the years ahead. It is a measured response to the changes emerging in the industry.

## Three Response Profiles

By creating an experiment to probe the periphery, Carmon chose the middle way of three prototypical responses to ambiguous signals.[3]

1. *Watch and wait.* This passive approach is appropriate when there is a high uncertainty due to conflicting information or if the firm has the resources to be a fast follower and let others lead. Watch and wait is often a good approach when there is no strong first-mover advantage and the risks of action are very high. It is also more appropriate if the potential costs of inaction are low.

2. *Probe and learn.* As uncertainty decreases or the cost of inaction increases, a more proactive approach is needed. This can range from focused market explorations with advanced research methods to the negotiation of option agreements to ensure the rights of first refusal to an emerging technology. The basic idea is to acquire a carefully balanced portfolio of strategic options to stay in the game and not be frozen out by competitive moves or external events.

3. *Believe and lead.* Full-scale commitment is warranted when the opportunity is very promising or the threat is imminent and when there are advantages to acting ahead of rivals. This more aggressive response is justified if a convergence of signals from the periphery occurs that supports the case for bold action. It also requires a full recognition of the risks of acting on fuzzy input from the periphery, to avoid mirages or futile battles with windmills.

These three prototypical strategies fall along a continuum. The focus of this chapter is on the probing and learning approach, especially on real options to enhance exploration. The next chapter explores the believe and lead strategy for action, especially the options that exploit clear opportunities. Naturally, the two are linked.

## Use Scenarios to Probe for Implications

To understand the changes in the business environment and their implications for the funeral business, Carmon's first step was to explore where the various weak signals might lead. This required identifying a full range of signals and then mapping out a variety of viewpoints or stories (scenarios) that would highlight key uncertainties in strategic ways. Carmon proposed that the National Funeral Directors Association (NFDA), for which he served as chairman, undertake such an endeavor to help its members adapt to change. During a two-day workshop with nearly one hundred industry leaders, participants sketched out four potential scenarios for the future of the funeral industry. These scenarios ranged from moderate changes in consumer preferences and gradual industry changes to very dramatic changes in both preferences and structures, as summarized in figure 5-1.

These four industry scenarios serve several purposes. First, they provide a context for learning. As new pieces of information come in, they can be fit into a given scenario. Thus, new signals that might have been seen as random noise are set into a pattern. For example, an increase in the personalization of cell phones might have been dismissed as totally unrelated to the funeral business, but now it might be seen as another development toward the "total tributes" or "survival of the fittest" scenarios. Second, by monitoring these signals, leaders can sense more quickly when the likelihood of a given scenario is becoming stronger. This awareness can help crystallize

**FIGURE 5-1**

## Scenarios for the funeral industry

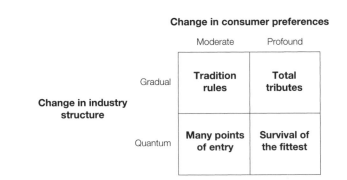

*Source*: Decision Strategies International, Inc. (DSI) and National Funeral Directors Association.

the picture, allowing the organization to act before rivals do or before windows of opportunity close. Third, the scenarios lay out competing assumptions about how the world is changing. Leaders can design experiments, such as Carmon's new center, that test some of these assumptions and thus accelerate the learning process. Carmon can now test the validity of different business models designed to capitalize on these different worlds. Finally, these experiments allow businesses to develop organizational capabilities that serve them well across multiple scenarios, so they can succeed no matter what the future brings.

## Examine the Business Impact

While experiments such as Carmon's new center provide insights into how the outside world is changing, he can also test new business models to jump the competition. The traditional funeral home business model stresses physical assets such as funeral parlors, hearses, and caskets. In addition to being stressed by the shift toward cremation, this business model is losing to an à la carte approach to purchasing funeral products and services. For example, Internet businesses offer caskets at an 80 percent discount, with delivery guaranteed in a few days. Price competition, rarely discussed in the past, has now become more open, with an unbundling of the fees for specific components. And as advances in information technology are increasing price transparency, they are also fueling an increase in remote participation in funeral services via video or the Internet, a revenue enhancer.

This kind of exploration of business implications can also help identify new rivals. The changes in the funeral industry might encourage consumers to look beyond the traditional funeral home to new competitors. For example, hospitals and hospices, institutions that are closest to the event of death, might assume some of the roles of the funeral home. Hotel chains that specialize in the celebration of life's pivotal moments—births, baptisms, weddings, and anniversaries—could easily add memorial celebrations. As part of their probing and learning, Carmon and other leaders should explore how various industry changes might open the door to nontraditional competitors. This kind of awareness could have helped telephone companies recognize the threats from cable companies, wireless companies, and other players as high-speed Internet access spread across the world.

Furthermore, the changes noted may have pivotal implications for human resources and business processes. As noted, Carmon hired an events planner. With more personalized services, the role of funeral director is changing from a person who *directs* to someone who *facilitates* highly customized funeral services. In the old model, the funeral director specifies how to conduct the viewing or the service, how the cars line up, and which route to take to the cemetery. But in some scenarios, this rather dictatorial role changes drastically in the direction of, say, a wedding planner, with the consumer in charge. The scenarios invite us to think through how a typical day in the life of a funeral home would differ across the four futures described and the ways that current practice might change. Such reflection, in turn, can lead to new insights about staffing, incentives, and organizational processes to capitalize on these changes.

The reason probing and learning is so critical is that the speed and nature of these scenarios will vary greatly by locale. Even general demographic trends, such as an aging population or an increase in the population of an ethnic group, will affect different towns or communities differently. A funeral home in a sophisticated, upscale neighborhood might welcome a radically new facility of the kind that John Carmon opened. But a funeral home serving a stable, strongly traditional neighborhood may choose to wait and see what happens with these shifts. Thus, business leaders must probe carefully in the context of their market and community for the true meaning of various weak signals.

## Searching More Broadly for Information

Sometimes a signal from the periphery will spark a broader search for information. For example, Matthew Simmons has been advising energy companies on mergers and acquisitions for over thirty-one years. He is well connected, and a few years back he paid a visit to Saudi Arabia on a government tour to learn more about that country's vast oil reserves. Although his fellow visitors were all very impressed with the presentations made by their Saudi hosts, Simmons was less impressed. In fact, he grew increasingly alarmed that the vast reserves the Saudi regime claimed to have had never been subjected to independent external review. And he really took notice when a senior manager at Aramco told the visitors that they were using advanced statistical techniques, such as fuzzy logic, to estimate the remaining oil reserves. Perhaps the term *fuzzy logic* didn't sit right with Simmons or some other pieces of the puzzle came together, but Simmons felt strongly that he must launch his own investigation. He had noticed something in the periphery that did not seem right. Now he needed to explore it further.[4]

Unfortunately, very little independent data, and only scant Saudi data, is published about the scope, history, and characteristics of the vast Saudi oil fields. There are many such fields, and the largest one, named Ghawar, accounts for nearly half of all Saudi oil production. This field has been producing for over fifty years with a cumulative output of 55 billion barrels of oil. It produces 5 million of the 85 million barrels the world eagerly consumes daily. Simmons knew that oil fields are notoriously temperamental and that, at most, only 40 percent of a reservoir can actually be harvested by pumping in water or gas to maintain the pressure. In Oman, a long-producing field operating at 960,000 barrels a day suddenly started to decline in 2001. What if this happened to Ghawar, that huge Saudi oil field the world depends on? Simmons found about two hundred scattered papers presented by Saudi petroleum engineers at various technical conferences around the world. Using this database, he developed predictive models of reservoir reserves and concluded that the Saudis had greatly overstated their reserves. Simmons's book *Twilight in the Desert: The Coming Saudi Oil Shock and the World Economy* contains the details while the title clearly conveys his message, which the Saudis and others vehemently dispute.[5]

Whether Simmons is ultimately proved right or wrong, executives like him must choose which weak signals of many to focus on when everything is still quite uncertain. This process may often begin with a hunch, but then lead to extensive fieldwork. And, of course, not all hunches will pay off. But once Simmons detected incongruent signals, he began probing for details that others failed to notice or had dismissed. Such smart and vigilant pursuits of peripheral signals are what this chapter is all about.

## Design Experiments and Options

One of the best ways to probe and learn about the periphery is to design experiments that help reduce the uncertainty where it helps most. These experiments should test specific hypotheses and assumptions that are relevant to the business. An experiment such as Carmon's new Family Life Center offers the organization a window into a new world. It not only provides information but creates an option for the organization to expand its investments and build on this pilot based on market feedback. Investments in *real* options bear a strong parallel to *financial* options, in that a small investment creates an opportunity for later investments once uncertainty is reduced (see box, "Real Options").

For example, various pharmaceutical and diagnostic firms are closely tracking a research collaboration known as the Nanosystems Biology Alliance, which aims to build a nanolab. This is a computer chip, one square centimeter in size, that could sense ten thousand

# Real Options

While financial options are well known to managers, the term *real option* is used to signal that some strategic investments (which cannot be traded or arbitraged in financial markets) create risk-reward profiles that are very similar to financial options. The basic Idea is that a small investment today provides an option for further investments in the future, after uncertainty has been reduced. In the financial realm, a typical call option creates an opportunity but not a commitment to a given course. It allows an investor to bet bigger later. For example, an option on one hundred shares of common stock allows the investor to purchase the stock at a strike price within a defined period of time. If the stock rises above the strike price, the investor can effectively purchase the stock at a discount. If the stock falls or remains below the strike price, the investor has risked only the small price of the options rather than the entire investment in the stock. As the term "option" implies, the investor reserves the option to purchase the stock in the future but not the obligation to do so.

Real options serve a similar purpose strategically. For example, a company might bet modestly to understand a new technology or market, either by supporting research in its own lab or through an investment in a startup or a pilot launch. If the initiative is successful, the company then has a preagreed option to invest substantially in the development and commercialization of the technology. If the technology fails to deliver, the company has risked only the seed money it has put into the project. By using real options, the company keeps its upfront investments low while learning about the emerging technology and preserving some upside potential. *continued*

The real options framework offers an alternative to the more static assessment of investments based on net present value or other discounted cash flow approaches. These latter approaches assume that the cash flow risks are fixed and can be explicitly quantified, but this is often not the case, particularly when dealing with the periphery. The risks of a new technology or unproven product are not known and change over time, making accurate predictions of a discount rate a real shot in the dark. In contrast, thinking in terms of real options explicitly recognizes the value of probing and learning to gain a more accurate picture before making substantial investments.

Like financial options, real options increase flexibility. Real options allow the company to defer, expand, contract, terminate, or otherwise modify projects along the way. In effect, these options allow the organization to learn about the periphery through quick glances to the side to see if more attention is warranted. This helps companies keep an eye on peripheral issues that could change the game without diverting too much attention and other resources from the focal area.[a]

a. William Hamilton, "Managing Real Options," in *Wharton on Managing Emerging Technologies*, edited by G. S. Day and Paul J. H. Schoemaker, 271–288 (New York: John Wiley & Sons, 2000).

different proteins to detect signs of impending disease. This new diagnostic helps to identify malfunctioning molecular pathways that can be regulated with drugs. By making relatively small investments in the development of this technology, these companies reserve the option to invest substantially in its commercialization as the technology evolves. In essence, they are probing, learning, and creating options all at once.

## Invest to Learn

While investments in real options are eventually expected to have a real financial payoff, the biggest return in the short term consists of new knowledge and a better understanding of developments in the periphery. For example, the CIA created In-Q-Tel, a private, not-for-profit venture fund, as a particularly effective outpost in probing and learning about emerging technologies that might apply to its intelligence mission.[6] In-Q-Tel makes investments in technology startups, typically in conjunction with other investors. While the investments are expected to produce a payoff, the CIA is not primarily interested in making money. Of far greater interest is that these positions give the CIA a window on new technologies that might be important to its work. In-Q-Tel offers the CIA an opportunity to exploit various new technologies as they emerge.

For example, one of In-Q-Tel's early investments was in a Las Vegas–based company, SRD, which had created data analysis software to detect hidden relationships. The software was designed to help casinos thwart cheaters, but it had natural applications as well in making connections within the CIA's own data about terrorist networks and other potential threats. While Las Vegas gaming is a long way from the CIA headquarters in Virginia, In-Q-Tel helped it to spot this technology at the periphery. Through its investment, the CIA could learn more quickly about the software's implications and development.

## Use Options for Different Types of Learning

Real options can serve many purposes. Ian MacMillan and Rita Gunther McGrath describe a variety of real options in an "opportunity portfolio" that reflects the level of uncertainty in an emerging technology and the market (see figure 5-2). The purpose of this kind of matrix is to provide a framework for mapping, evaluating, and allocating

FIGURE 5-2

**The many uses of options**

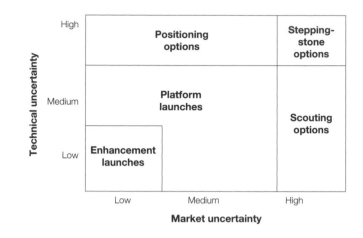

Source: Ian C. MacMillan and Rita Gunther McGrath, "Crafting R&D Project Porfolios," *Research Technology Management* (September–October 2002): 48–59.

resources to a mix of low- and high-risk technology investments. There are several types of options here that are particularly germane to the process of probing and learning:

- *Scouting options.* These are cautious investments made to discover or create markets, such as the venture capital investments of In-Q-Tel. The scouting metaphor from the military is apt: you send out scouts to find the enemy, and even if these scouts don't come back, the generals at least know the whereabouts of the enemy. These are small pilots used when the product or technology is relatively certain but the market is uncertain. Through small probing investments, the company learns about the marketplace without making the huge investments that accompany commercialization.

- *Positioning options.* These are cautious investments that preserve options when there is a clear market opportunity but many unproven products or business models. The aim is to spend a little to learn a lot. In the early evolution of mobile telephony or other technologies, for example, companies faced diverse standards and much uncertainty about which one would emerge as *the* standard. Given such uncertainty, a company might use real options to preserve a position in all the primary standards. Microsoft did this in the mid-1980s by investing across multiple platforms such as its own DOS, IBM's OS/2, and Apple's Macintosh operating system.[7] It could then move quickly once it became clear which standard was emerging as the winner or pursue multiple lines if there were no common standard.

- *Stepping-stone options.* These options entail high market and technical uncertainty, and so you must minimize fixed investments and sunk costs until you assure feasibility. These small exploratory forays help you to gain experience that you can use as stepping-stones. For example, Sanyo Corporation first developed solar cells for low-end applications such as wrist watches and calculators; early cells could easily power these products. With this experience in these low-end applications, the company refined the technology, resolved technological uncertainties, increased efficiency, and generated a modest income, allowing it to ultimately move to higher-end applications such as solar panels for factory heating. Through this series of stepping-stones, the company continued to expand its business in this area while learning about the technology.

More extensive investments move beyond probing and learning. These include platform options, such as Gillette's new razor technology, that create the option for further enhancements. They are most appropriate when the weak signals have become strong enough for you to lay a sizable bet. There are also enhancement launches based on existing platforms. Again, with less market uncertainty, these are less for probing and learning than for acting to exploit a clear opportunity.

MacMillan and McGrath develop a related framework that can aid in learning from options. Discovery-driven planning helps identify, test, and track assumptions for uncertain ventures. A new investment is viewed here as a series of assumptions—some explicit and many implicit—that must be tested as quickly as possible. Rather than waiting for these assumptions to be validated or proven false in the normal course of business, managers can choose some critical ones that can be accelerated and tested sooner through a deliberate discovery process, akin to probing in specific areas for key insights. For example, one of their tools, called the "reverse income statement," forces managers to identify the key assumptions underlying their financial target returns. These assumptions can in turn be tracked or related to key milestones that are necessary to reach these goals. This type of framework can help managers better see the financial implications of various assumptions for the business and learn faster about what works and doesn't. Also, it allows managers to be more decisive about when to pull the plug or accelerate investments.[8]

## Seeking Serendipity

In addition to helping to test hypotheses, any experiment may offer unexpected insights, as DuPont found when it experimented in the biosciences, which present a potentially rich but highly uncertain set of opportunities for DuPont. New technologies could transform biomass waste such as corn husks into a valuable replacement for petroleum or create diverse biomaterials. But which ones will actually pay off?

"There are a remarkable number of biological assets to consider, select, and invest in," said Dr. John Ranieri, vice president and general manager of DuPont Bio-Based Materials.[9] "Our challenge is: How do we achieve knowledge intensity and put these pieces together?

This is where we start asking questions in different and smarter ways—which can generate a lot of pleasant surprises. Actually if you are not being surprised, then you're not asking the right questions, because in this environment, you should be surprised."

DuPont has used real options to explore this uncertain area of the periphery. To develop biomass technologies, it created a joint $40 million project with the U.S. government. To explore biomaterials, DuPont made more than a dozen investments in areas such as sustainable materials and energy, applied biosurfaces, and therapeutics. "We kept asking, how do we reduce the uncertainty? How do we get a platform we can build on?"

This focus on low-cost learning led DuPont to identify investment opportunities around the world. For example, one project proposed using organisms called methanotropes to develop highly valued chemicals, but the process required a lot of methane and a fermenter to implement. DuPont found a company in Norway that had already built a fermenter to handle methane generated as a by-product of oil production, and it created an alliance. Combining DuPont's software with the Norwegian hardware allowed DuPont to test the concept without making massive investments.

"We use real options thinking to help frame our investments in the early stages when technologies and markets are not yet fully formed," Ranieri said. "This is the phase when not enough is known to apply traditional measures like NPV [net present value]." This approach helps DuPont to avoid overspending on projects by keeping early investments low and pulling the plug as soon as it is clear that the technology will not be successful.

DuPont recognizes that, at the periphery, there is always much that is not known, so the best approach is to keep early investments small and learn as quickly as possible to reduce the uncertainty. This allows the organization to test hypotheses and also invites unexpected insights. As Ranieri said, "We found some things that were expected, but we found that some of the most interesting ones were in the surprises." As they conduct experiments, managers must prepare for and learn from such surprises. Learning creates opportunities for serendipity.

## Make Deliberate Mistakes

While most experiments are designed to test a critical assumption expected to be true, sometimes companies can use deliberate mistakes to probe more broadly.[10] The strategy of erring deliberately tests key propositions expected to be false. For example, advertising pioneer David Ogilvy deliberately included ads that he thought would fail in his tests. Most did, but occasionally there were some pleasant surprises. His approach was not aimed at testing just the ads themselves but especially his entire framework or viewpoint about advertising. Ogilvy could detect new shifts in the market, and society at large, before his rivals because he viewed his strategy as nothing but a bunch of flawed hypotheses. Credit card companies are now routinely accepting consumers whom they would normally reject just to test their models.

These types of deliberate mistakes can have big payoffs in the long run. Before the breakup of the Bell System, U.S. telephone companies were required to offer service to any new subscriber in their region. Throughout the United States, there were about 12 million new subscribers each year, with an annual bad debt exceeding $450 million. To protect against this credit risk, as well against equipment abuse by customers, each Bell operating company was permitted by law to force a small percentage of subscribers to pay a security deposit. Which ones should be chosen? Each company had developed its own complex statistical model for requesting a deposit from the right set of customers—those deemed the greatest credit risks. But even though the companies were making optimal decisions according to their current models, they never really knew if the models themselves were right. They decided to test this by making a deliberate, multimillion-dollar mistake.

For almost a year, the Bell companies didn't ask for a deposit from nearly 100,000 customers randomly selected from those who were considered high credit risks. It was clearly a mistake not to demand a security deposit from these customers because some surely would not pay their bills or would run off with the equipment. The Bell companies knew the move would cost them many more millions in lost equipment and unpaid bills. But the companies were humble enough about what they didn't know to study how these high-credit-risk customers actually compared with the rest of the population.

To their surprise, quite a few of the presumed "bad" customers actually paid their bills fully and on time. And some of the "bad" customers did not damage or steal the phones and related equipment as much as the "good" customers. Armed with these new insights, the companies recalibrated their credit-scoring model and instituted a much smarter screening strategy, which added $137 million to their bottom line every year for the next decade. It proved a very profitable mistake. By deliberately erring in the first year, the companies obtained the missing information needed to choose more wisely in subsequent years.[11] In essence, they probed the shadows of their knowledge base.

While most experiments test a specific hypothesis that is assumed to be true, the strategy of deliberate mistakes clearly tests hypotheses that are presumed to be false but that (in case they happen to be true) could change the entire mental model. If we really want to probe the periphery effectively, we must balance positive testing (for things we assume to be true—the Bell companies example) with negative testing (for things we assume to be false—David Ogilvy's loser ads). Companies often recognize the value of learning from inadvertent mistakes, but seldom do they probe deeply by blundering deliberately.

Of course, anyone can goof up repeatedly and continually, jumping from a roof to see whether it really hurts, and so we must choose strategically among the mistakes we actually commit. No organization should make mistakes all the time, but deliberate mistakes clearly help us explore the periphery, where we must sort many false beliefs from the correct ones. By looking more broadly at the issues, you can expand your opportunities, probe the world around you, and challenge your own thinking. As James Joyce wrote, mistakes "are the portals of discovery."

## Conclusion: The Quick and the Dead

Learning quickly and efficiently is vital in responding to the periphery. Organizations that can gain clarity about what is happening before their rivals will be in a better position to act on opportunities in the periphery or respond to threats. As noted in this chapter, learning can be improved and accelerated by the following approaches:

- *Use scenarios to learn.*  Scenarios not only help interpret the future but they can also help in probing and learning. They organize signals that may seem to be random noise into a pattern. They show where knowledge and insights are needed, and they help companies explore the business implications of different futures.[12]

- *Fail fast and cheap to accelerate learning.*  Experiments can be the best way to learn about the periphery. Keep them as small as possible to extract the most learning with the least risk. While good peripheral vision is important in identifying opportunities, the real value of the periphery is to explore mistakes.

- *Use real options.*  One of the best ways to increase the learning-to-risk ratio is to use real options. Options can turn small investments into powerful learning opportunities. They can help to reduce uncertainty before major investments are required. The idea is to keep the upfront investment low while learning and preserving the upside potential.

The resources an organization devotes to learning and the speed with which it moves depend on its context. For example, John Carmon and his colleagues in the funeral business have the luxury of more time than managers in most industries. "We are definitely an industry that is steeped in tradition and slow to change," Carmon said. "This is a generational shift." Even so, in a drastically changing environment, he must probe and learn quickly to prepare for new futures that might emerge. Carmon is proactively doing so by designing experiments and options to better understand the changes at the periphery of this particular business environment. If and when the picture becomes clearer as a result of this learning, Carmon will probably be ready to seize the opportunities before others do. The new Family Life Center is not only a learning platform but a platform for growth, the first step toward acting on new signals from the periphery. Acting aggressively on signals from the periphery presents its own challenges, as discussed in the next chapter.

# Chapter Six

# Acting

## What to Do with These Insights

*"Writing is like driving at night in the fog.*
*You can only see as far as your headlights,*
*but you can make the whole trip that way."*

—E. L. Doctorow

NSIDE A SMALL open briefcase on the desk of a senior executive in the lighting industry is a set of flat white plastic
panels. With the twist of a few dials, he can adjust the blue light-
emitting diode (LED) panels in the box so they gradually shift closer
to white light. The upper limit is still a bluish white glow that most
homebuilders wouldn't choose for living space, but it keeps getting
closer to pure white every year. This gradual movement toward
white light may be the greatest threat confronting the lighting business since the invention of the incandescent bulb. The promise of

white LED light has emboldened solid-state lighting pioneer Shuji Nakamura to state, "I want to replace all conventional lighting."[1] But as the executive turns the dials, he wonders, How quickly will Nakamura's vision become a reality?

The LED is poised to transform the $15 billion general-illumination market in the same way that transistors (replacing vacuum tubes) transformed the electronics industry or CDs transformed the music industry. This solid-state lighting (SSL) is the first truly new lighting technology to emerge in nearly a century. While the LED was invented in the 1960s, more recent breakthroughs in color and increasing intensity (lumens) have moved this technology from calculator displays and indicator lamps into much broader applications.

The most dramatic sign of this technology's transition from novelty item to competitive threat was the loss of the U.S. traffic-light market to LEDs. A red LED signal light operates on 90 percent less energy than the 150-watt incandescent light it replaces, with a longer life.[2] The economics are remarkable, with a payback period for replacement of less than one year and an annual savings of more than $1,000 per intersection. U.S. federal regulations require that all traffic signals switch to SSL by 2006, virtually eliminating a market of about $1 billion annually for traditional bulbs.

Adding insult to injury, MIT's *Technology Review* proclaimed in 2003 that the incandescent light was one of the top ten technologies "that deserved to die."[3] Suddenly the technology that had been at the heart of industry with minor modifications since the time Thomas Edison watched the glow of his first filament is facing possible extinction. The $15 billion U.S. illumination industry is now in the crosshairs of a new set of rivals using solid-state technology, which offers many advantages over traditional lighting (see box, "The Advantages of Solid-State Lighting"). It may be a life-threatening challenge to traditional players such as Philips Lighting,

# The Advantages of Solid-State Lighting

The advantages of SSL are many. LEDs are basically semiconductors that convert electricity into light more efficiently than conventional light sources. In addition to reducing energy consumption, SSL's low voltage makes it safer and more easily powered by solar energy or batteries. Because there is no filament to break, SSL is more durable and consequently has a much longer life with lower maintenance costs. Whereas conventional lights can only be turned off, on, or dimmed, the LED is much more versatile; it can change colors or flash in response to software commands. In traditional lighting, the fixtures are permanent and the bulbs are changed. With SSL, many sources of light can be integrated into products that are sealed for life. While traditional technologies have progressed over the past two centuries, including the advent of fluorescent and high-intensity discharge lighting, they appear to have plateaued at efficiencies of below 25 percent. In contrast, energy conversion efficiencies of greater than 50 percent have been achieved in solid-state devices in the infrared spectrum, and researchers expect to make similar breakthroughs in diodes emitting white light. If these levels can be achieved, scientists believe that SSL will provide a 150–200 lumen/watt light source that is twice as efficient as fluorescent lighting and ten times more efficient than incandescent lamps.[a] This would fundamentally transform the lighting industry.

a. lighting.sandia.gov/Xlightingoverview.htm.

GE, and Osram Sylvania in their core markets for commercial and residential illumination.

Even before this new threat emerged, the industry was facing serious challenges that may have distracted managers from paying closer attention to LEDs. The average selling price of lightbulbs had declined by approximately 10 percent between 2000 and 2003.[4] The U.S. consumer and professional lightbulb markets collectively lost about $500 million in value in the same period, shrinking from $2.9 billion to $2.4 billion as a result of commoditization and intense price competition. Incumbents had to keep their eyes on this low-cost, commodity game. With the rapid advances in the technology of SSL, however, they must look elsewhere as well.

Now that the lighting executives have recognized the threat from the periphery (and it is becoming less peripheral every day), what should they do? Acting is integrally related to the process of probing and learning (discussed in the previous chapter). But the focus of probing is primarily on *learning*, while the focus of acting is on *exploiting* opportunities or *avoiding* threats from the periphery.

## Strategies for Acting Under Uncertainty

The challenge for acting is that there is still great ambiguity and uncertainty. How quickly will the technology emerge? How fast will the market adopt it? What twists and turns might it take? While the threat is clearly on the horizon and SSL looks like a winner in the long run, managers also must make profits in the short run. If adoption is slower than expected, incumbents might find themselves like Jack in the old tale, trading an uncertain promise of a few magic beans for a cash-cow business that still can be milked for many years to come. If the managers move too slowly, however, pioneers such as Nakamura are ready to conquer the market.

When companies recognize an opportunity, they often must move quickly to capitalize on it (see box, "Apple Quickly Opens Its i"). While there may not be time for the extensive probing and learning discussed in the previous chapter, companies can use small launches to create platforms for future growth. Companies can also collaborate with others to move more quickly while sharing the risk or to expand the scope of their competitive monitoring to act more broadly.

## Use Many Small Launches: A Thousand Points of Light

Many small initiatives can help to create opportunities while keeping risks small. As noted in the previous chapter, these experiments can be used to probe and learn, but as they become successful, they also create platforms for action. For example, Philips launched a number of initiatives that provide hands-on experience with emerging technologies such as SSL, from launching LED candles to creating ambient lighting systems for hospitals. "We have used a launch-and-learn strategy to better understand solid-state lighting, as well as try out new business models," said Govi Rao, a vice president at Philips Lighting.[5] "These experiments allow us to monitor many factors such as channel conflicts or cannibalization effects. This is where incumbent companies are often blindsided. By creating pilots, we minimize risks. If we make mistakes, we keep them small and learn quickly." Philips designed various launches to test different aspects of the emerging solid-state world—one, for example, looked at applying a solid-state solution to retrofit traditional lighting technologies (new bulbs for old sockets); another used SSL in a radically different model for lighting using ambient lighting panels.

The first example was the launch of Philips's Aurelle LED candle. It provides a light similar to a candle but without the risks and inconvenience of open flames. "The Aurelle candle is not the typical

# Apple Quickly Opens Its i

Sometimes, there isn't much time for probing and learning, so companies must learn from the experiments of others. Apple used its awareness of the experiments of Napster and other file-sharing services, as well as its own acquisitions, to quickly gain the knowledge needed to launch iPod. Even so, Steve Jobs almost missed the revolution. He is one of the most perceptive technology leaders in recent history, having recognized the power of the mouse and graphical user interface that became the Macintosh and the potential for computer animation that led to Pixar. But in the summer of 2000, Jobs was very focused on perfecting the Mac's capabilities for video editing and he almost didn't recognize one of the biggest music revolutions in the digital world. "I felt like a dope," he said later in an interview with *Fortune*. "I thought we had missed it. We had to work hard to catch up."[a]

lighting product we are used to, and it challenges all our systems and thinking—from design and product development to channel development and marketing," Rao said. "We had to adjust our way of working significantly and move faster than expected as this product quickly became very popular." This was a real product in a real market, and, as sales took off, it moved from an experiment to a viable business. If it had failed, however, the risks to the company were low. Because it is uncertain which actions will have payoffs, the goal is often to invest in many small experiments and then add support to those that are successful.

When Jobs recognized the shift, Apple acted quickly. It immediately added CD burners to all its computers. Jobs then purchased a small company, SoundStep, run by a former Apple software engineer, to jumpstart its software development. Apple
created the first version of iTunes in four months and produced the
first iPod player nine months later. The company still needed content to put on its iPods, and it worked out agreements with major
record companies to develop a platform for selling the songs.

Fortunately for Jobs, the music industry was so busy suing
Napster and its own customers that he had more time than he realized. When Apple's iTunes Music Store opened in April 2003, the
goal was to sell a million songs in six months. It crossed the million
mark in just six days. By early 2005, iTunes controlled 62 percent
of all legal digital music downloads and iPod accounted for more
than half of MP3 players, despite aggressive competition.

a. In Brent Schendler, "How Big Can Apple Get?" *Fortune*, February 21, 2005, 38–45.

As part of this portfolio of experiments, some will not have an
immediate payoff. For example, a lighting environment installed in
an urban hospital explored more far-reaching applications of SSL. It
explored opportunities not only to replace bulbs in existing sockets
but also to change the entire infrastructure and paradigm of lighting.
"The entire value chain is built around building and filling sockets,"
Rao said. "Solid-state lighting completely changes that paradigm.
You can now create light without having sockets."

To explore this socketless world, Philips created an experiment with ambient lighting at Chicago's Lutheran General Hospital.

Philips designed and implemented a new pediatric cardiology pavilion that integrates ambient lighting technology into projection and LED lighting panels. Young patients can choose one of four different themes: aquatic, space, fly-through, or a default lava lamp. The choices are coded on RFID cards carried by the patients, so the theme and lighting change as they enter the room. The ambient environment enhances the setting as well as the procedures. For example, if a child must hold her breath during a procedure, an otter in an aquatic scene might do the same to set an example.

Both experiments tested not only the technology but also new business models, value chains, and market reactions. All of this helped to illuminate the potential of this new market space. "We are learning by doing and create strategic options based on what we've learned," Rao said. "The value of such experiments lies in our ability to challenge the current paradigm of doing business and this is exactly what we accomplished with these two experiments. I would like to have at least half a dozen of these experiments, quickly, to act on the learning."

The initial experiments are often in markets where the benefits of LED lighting outweigh its limitations. In situations where it is difficult to change lightbulbs, the longer life of SSL, which can last about fifty times longer than a 60-watt bulb, offers a natural advantage. For example, Osram Sylvania is developing long strips of flexible, adhesive-tape-covered LEDs for use on the outside of buildings or swimming pools, where changing bulbs is challenging or time-consuming.[6]

## Collaborate with Others

Because the target in mining the LED periphery is fairly clear and affects the entire lighting industry, it seemed advantageous to join forces with other firms to explore it. This approach increases resources and reduces risks. Companies in the lighting industry joined together to create an initiative called Bridges in Light. In 2003, the major stakeholders came together to map the future of the industry, and the leaders in the industry created a "burning platform" to drive industry change and used this platform to develop wide-ranging scenarios for the future. This initiative continues and is currently being coordinated under the auspices of the National Electrical Manufacturers Association (NEMA), where it is being evaluated as a marketing program for the industry.

Joint ventures also allow the incumbent to gain access to new capabilities relating to issues such as semiconductor manufacturing models, pace of innovation, access to global markets, and protection of intellectual property. Because SSL requires these different capabilities, many incumbents entered into joint ventures. Lumileds was originally set up by Philips and Agilent Technologies around 2000 to design and manufacture LEDs. GELcore, a partnership between GE and semiconductor firm Emcore, is also making LEDs. These and other partnerships give the incumbents a platform for acting on the technology as it develops and participating in it as it becomes a more significant part of the industry.

## Act More Broadly

Companies often must expand their field of action to embrace more of the periphery. For example, in lighting, incumbents viewed the entire value chain more broadly to develop strategies for action. The traditional value chain is shown in figure 6-1. With the end consumers focused more on price, companies are fighting an increasingly tough battle in what has essentially become a commodity business. They are trying to influence the original equipment manufacturers (OEMs), specifiers/designers, and contractors who choose lighting for end consumers. With brutal price wars and battles for shelf space and mind share among specifiers and designers, there is plenty to focus on in this picture. But this narrow scope obscures

**FIGURE 6-1**

**Narrow view of lighting industry**

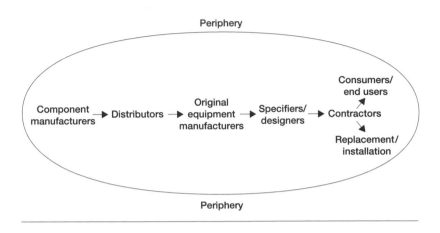

important parts of the picture. The companies should ask, What significant forces and factors lie outside this typical view of the value chain and how could they transform our industry?

A much broader lighting ecosystem, as shown in figure 6-2, could accelerate the emergence of SSL or slow its progress. For example, the spread of SSL will depend on technology, changes in customers' buying behavior and needs, and perhaps regulations. The development of the new technology may also be affected by a variety of other forces, including health, security, energy (load management and demand/response), transportation, coordinated research, aesthetics, sustainable development, and "dark-sky" environmental issues. Managers should look at these different areas and act where needed. Let's consider a few examples:

- *Development of technology.* The industry needs to assess technological changes, particularly innovations that can lead to the development of high-quality white light and reductions in cost. Projections of prices for solid-state technology between 2000 and 2020 range from $14 per kilolumen to as

FIGURE 6-2

## Broader lighting ecosystem

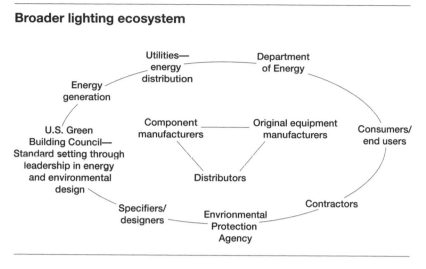

low as 50 cents per kilolumen, and efficacy estimates range from four to eight times that of incandescent lighting.[7] This is a very broad range, and it means that the new technology could swallow anywhere from 10 to 90 percent of the current market for incandescent and fluorescent lights. Clearly the periphery in this area is very cloudy, so lighting companies must invest in developing technology or supporting research, particularly those that reduce costs or increase efficiency.

- *Changes in the attitudes of trade and end users.* While the technology can facilitate adoption, the willingness of contractors and end users to adopt this new technology will be a rate-limiting factor in the spread of SSL. About one-third of the total lumen-hour demand is replaced or installed in any one year, which limits the maximum penetration rate of a new technology. Managers must develop a strategy for addressing both contractors and end users, as well as the emergence of intermediaries such as designers and specifiers, who influence lighting decisions. This requires a broader market and channels strategy and an expanded set of actions.

- *Lobbying and public affairs.* Attitudes toward conservation and energy consumption will have a significant impact on the industry. These attitudes will be reflected in both market perceptions of the technology and government regulations. The impact of such regulations can already be seen in the use of LEDs in traffic lights. According to U.S. Department of Energy forecasts, widespread adoption of SSL could reduce the worldwide consumption of electricity for lighting by more than 50 percent, resulting in a 10 percent decrease in overall electricity consumption. Increasing environmental concerns about energy consumption, carbon emissions and mercury pollution, and other issues could accelerate the move to SSL. Managers must deal proactively with government and the media through lobbying, public affairs, and other strategies for shaping these policies in ways that do the least damage to their competitive positions and sustain the long-term health of the industry.

- *Preparing for the wild cards.* Another peripheral issue that may affect SSL is the relationship between lighting and health. Neonatal researchers have shown that premature babies respond better under certain LED lighting conditions. Also, lighting is used to treat seasonal affective disorder (SAD), mood swings related to seasonal changes in sunlight. On the other hand, there may be negative impacts of light on health. For example, researchers have studied possible links between exposure to light at night and increased reports of breast cancer and colorectal cancer, but at this point this is more of a red herring.[8] There is also growing concern about light "pollution" in urban areas, with the dark-sky movement campaigning for changes in public and private illumination to create darker, more natural skies. Managers must monitor these issues carefully and prepare for such wild cards as a breakthrough in the use of lighting in medicine or a negative study that sends a chill through the industry. First actions might include studying the issues, establishing relationships with healthcare players, and influencing the debate about dark skies.

A lighting company's strategies must consider this broader perspective of rivals, customers, and the environment. This will require a set of balanced actions in the broader arena just described, with a careful eye on costs and benefits. The challenge is especially how to balance the traditional investment mind-set of the known space with the real options approach of the unknown arena.

## Limits of First-mover Advantages

One of the arguments often cited for quick, bold action is to gain a first-mover advantage. It may appear that the lion's share of the new wealth goes to the first mover. Managers may want only a gold medal, not silver nor bronze. The profits, they believe, go to those companies that actively sense the early signals, anticipate the threats or opportunities ahead of rivals, and move without hesitation. And, in theory, the first mover gets to shape the rules of competition by preempting slower-moving rivals, locking up the best positions and channels, and gaining an unassailable leadership position in the minds of consumers.

The empirical evidence, however, provides a more complex picture of first-mover advantages. The benefits are realized only by the pioneers that survive. And even then, being first does not automatically bestow an advantage; it only provides an opportunity.[9] Long-term resource commitments demand courage and a clear vision of a mass market opportunity and relentless innovation before the advantage is secured. But very few of the true pioneers survive to lead markets. Instead, most of the long-term rewards go to fast well-funded followers who learn from the pioneers. For example, neither Kimberly-Clark nor Procter & Gamble pioneered the disposable diaper market, but they quickly came to dominate it. GE did not create the CAT scanner market, but it extracted the profits.

Being a smart fast follower requires very strong peripheral vision. The pivotal event to watch for in the establishment of a new market is the emergence of a dominant design. This is defined as the standard that sets the product features and benefits and that commands the support of the early buyers. It provides a platform from which spring a wide range of variants that are not fundamentally different. Once buyers, suppliers, and competitors coalesce around the design, a major source of uncertainty is eliminated. Fast followers often wait for a dominant design to begin to emerge and then move quickly to enter and be a part of the development of the market.[10] This means being as ready to move as quickly as any first mover—by having the technology in hand, the product design ready, and market and manufacturing plans in place. Typically, there is a sharp inflection point when a dominant design emerges. Not being prepared to act usually means missing the window of opportunity and being relegated to a slow follower. (One expensive and risky way to overcome this delayed start is to acquire a promising pioneer and spend heavily.)

So, in fast following, timing is everything. Listed next are some of the indicators that a company needs to follow fast (as proposed by Constantinos Markides and Paul Geroski):

- *A slowdown in the rate of technological and business model innovation.* The variants offered in succeeding generations of development are becoming more similar.

- *A growing sense of legitimacy.* In effect, the market has "crossed the chasm" from early enthusiasts who will put up with many deficiencies to engage the majority of potential consumers.[11]

- *The appearance of complementary goods producers.* These players provide essential services including market access and are well informed about the prospects for the market.[12]

Being a fast follower also offers the company more time to probe and learn. Successful fast followers must watch the periphery and carefully monitor the leading indicators of an emerging dominant design. They must learn along with the pioneers, even while acting more slowly. But because fast followers delay their investments and action, they face decreased risks as they learn more about an uncertain future.

## Knowing When to Learn or Leap

When uncertainty is very high or opportunities to create options and experiments are limited, the best course may be "watch and wait." Investor Warren Buffet looked foolish on the sidelines while all those dot-coms and IPOs were experiencing fabulous stock price appreciations. But his rationale was simple and compelling: "I don't invest in things I don't understand." Time proved him right.

Ultimately, the wisdom of this and other strategies depends on a risk-reward calculation. How should managers decide how aggressively to respond to a signal? Several factors affect the choice.

- *The availability of flexible options.* To create and exercise strategic options, you need opportunities to do so. Some industries and environments present numerous opportunities for such options, whereas other environments offer relatively few possibilities. If options can be used, this can significantly reduce the costs of acting and learning as the periphery becomes clearer. But in other cases, it is an all-or-nothing proposition. Sometimes organizations can create new structures and initiatives that expand opportunities for options, such as the CIA's development of In-Q-Tel.

- *The ambiguity of the signals.* The ratio of uncertainty to knowledge is a key factor in deciding whether to act on signals. The higher the uncertainty, the greater the need to learn more and reduce it. As uncertainty is reduced through probing and learning, there may be a stronger case for action.

- *The cost and reversibility of action.* The absolute cost of a course of action will also affect choices. If the cost of a given strategic action is relatively low, it will be easier to act in an ambiguous environment. If the cost is high relative to the potential return, more caution is called for. An important component of cost is the ease of undoing the decision. If the cost of reversibility is high, most expenditures will become sunk costs.

- *Opportunities to learn.* Some environments offer few opportunities to learn, so investments in a probe and learn strategy may just defer a difficult decision. Managers must clearly identify what they are trying to learn from their experiments and whether they can actually do so. When they cannot reduce ambiguity further, then they must act or exit.

- *The risks of standing still.* If there is a high risk associated with standing still—for example, when competitors are actively positioning to move on the same opportunities— a bolder strategy may be required, especially if first-mover advantages exist. The risks of standing still should always be formally examined because the status quo will seldom remain as it is.

- *The upside potential.* Just as costs matter, so do benefits. What is the upside potential of moving early and preempting rivals? Is this a case where setting standards or locking up partners is important? Might there be snowballing effects or tipping-point dynamics at play? Various conceptual frameworks can help assess the benefits (and costs) of being a first or earlier mover.[13] A simple framework is to determine the value of an "uncontested market day," the revenue the company would earn if it owned the market for a day, and then multiply that by the number of days before significant rivals might enter. It is a broad-brush estimate, but it can provide an order-of-magnitude assessment of the upside potential.

But before taking a bold approach, you should be careful to ask yourself whether there are less dramatic options that might reduce the risks or have a better chance of success. Can real options be created? Have you tested your key assumptions? Can scenarios lead to other options? What are the risks of putting all your eggs in one basket? Are the signals really clear enough or could they mean something else? What can be learned from experiments that have already been undertaken by other companies? If, after this testing, action is still called for, you sometimes must simply leap.

## Driving Through the Fog

Acting on peripheral vision is often like Doctorow's image of driving through fog. Managers must proceed step by step. While they need a long-term vision, they also must recognize that much of the landscape is still obscured. It will unfold as a result of each successive mile as they move down the road. Each action sets up the next.

As the environment becomes clearer, investments can be made with greater confidence and actions can be more decisive. Until that point, the focus should be on reducing the uncertainty and preserving opportunities. The goal is to fill in a blurry, colorless, and indistinct signal with missing detail, through a process of sideways glances and a series of small actions. In the words of Govi Rao of Philips, "launch and learn." The light at the end of the tunnel may emerge as an opening to a new market or an oncoming train—or both, as the traditional lighting industry discovered. When companies act, they begin to add their own signals to the environment and uniquely organize the patterns around them.

To successfully travel through the fog of the periphery requires the right vehicle. Organizations can build capabilities that facilitate and support peripheral vision. The next chapter considers the factors that can help organizations better navigate the fog at the periphery.

# Chapter Seven

# Organizing

## How to Develop Vigilance

*"It is difficult to look further than you can see."*

—*Winston Churchill*

MATTEL'S BARBIE appeared to be unstoppable. The doll had renewed itself time and again for more than four decades since its launch in 1959—as doctor, astronaut, and even presidential candidate—selling more than 1 billion dolls and creating the most valuable toy brand in the world. But age eventually caught up with Barbie—not her own, but the age compression of her young customers. Girls were growing up more quickly and losing interest in Barbie at an earlier age. The industry was further squeezed by an advancing tide of computer and video games that were absorbing more of the time of these busy young girls. The core market for Barbie dolls was compressed from ages three to eleven down to three to five. These shifts at the periphery created a major challenge for Mattel and an attractive opportunity for rivals, as shown in figure 7-1.

In 2001, the MGA Entertainment Company seized this opportunity, launching its hip new Bratz doll line. It targeted the precocious older girls who were defecting from Barbie (see box, "Battle for the Valley of the Dolls"). Bratz dolls looked like their teenage siblings and the pop stars they idolized. Within three years, the company had sold more than 80 million Bratz dolls, and Bratz had become the top lifestyle brand for girls ages seven to fourteen.[1] In 2004, Bratz sales had climbed to $700 million while Barbie's sales had been frozen at about $1.5 billion, and Mattel's share of the fashion-doll market shrank by 20 percent between 2001 and 2004.[2] In addition to eroding Barbie's share in the United States, Bratz also gained share in the United Kingdom, controlling more than 30 percent of the fashion doll market there by 2004.[3]

The erosion of Mattel's fashion doll franchise was far from a peripheral concern for Mattel, which depended on Barbie sales for

FIGURE 7-1

**Squeezing Barbie's core market**

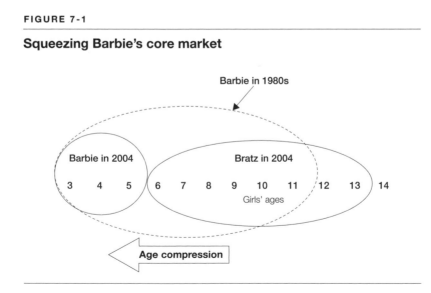

# Battle for the Valley of the Dolls

What made Bratz dolls so successful? Part of the reason is that they look more like the streetwise teenagers that younger girls admire, satisfying their yearning for maturity. Barbie, with carriages and fairy-tale outfits, appeals to the childhood fantasy popular with three to five-year-old girls, while Bratz depicts pouty-lipped teenagers with an attitude (see the accompanying figure). Bratz creator Isaac Larian contends that very young girls look to Barbie as a mother figure but turn to older girls for role models as they

grow up.[a] While Barbie's look is mainstream, the Bratz look is multicultural, and Bratz pays careful attention to fashion and makeup.

a. "The Queen Is Dead," *The Guardian*, October 6, 2004, http://shopping.guardian-co.uk/toys/story/0,1587,1320801,00.html.

30–40 percent of its operating profits.[4] Mattel moved aggressively after the fact to try to rescue Barbie's declining fortunes. A full fourteen months after the Bratz launch Mattel came out with a brand extension for Barbie targeting older girls (My Scene) and a me-too line of hip dolls called Flavas to compete directly with Bratz. Research by Robert Cooper shows that such me-too brands typically have only a 28 percent success rate, compared with 82 percent for unique and superior products.[5] (Note that the plodding and uncreative imitators in this study are not the same as the fast followers discussed in the previous chapter.) Mattel's Flavas brand did not meet expectations and was discontinued in 2004.[6] None of Mattel's moves was sufficient to stop Barbie's loss of one-fifth of her realm in a few years.

Strong peripheral vision is not just the result of occasional brilliance in scoping, scanning, interpretation, probing, and acting, as discussed in the previous chapters. It is above all the result of a capacity that the organization can develop and strengthen. What were the organizational weaknesses that made it harder for Mattel to recognize and react to the changes in its environment? What capabilities are most important for organizations in building their peripheral vision? What distinguishes the organizations that have this capability (vigilant organizations) from those that do not (vulnerable organizations)?

## Five Components of a Capability for Peripheral Vision

Our research has identified five components of peripheral vision capability that are particularly important for an organization to be consistently good at sensing the periphery:

1. Vigilant leadership that encourages a broad focus on the periphery.

2. An inquisitive approach to strategy development.

3. A flexible and inquisitive culture that rewards exploring the edge.

4. Knowledge systems for detecting and sharing weak signals.

5. An organizational configuration and processes that encourage the exploration of the periphery.

In our survey of senior executives, leadership was far and away the most significant factor, followed by incentives and a configuration that encourages the sharing of information and an interest in the periphery (see appendix A). An organization with leaders that have a limited and myopic attitude toward the world beyond its borders, in which few people care about the edges of the business, will have less effective peripheral vision than an organization that is active and curious and practices systematic scanning and probing.

Capabilities for peripheral vision are related to *how* the organization senses and acts, rather than to *what* it does, so they might be considered meta-capabilities of the organization that cut across the operational capabilities.[7] The capabilities that contribute to peripheral vision tend to be broader than some of the more operationally focused competencies relating to areas such as internal production, customer service, or alliance management. These meta-capabilities will probably be overlooked or underdeveloped amid the daily demands of the business. Many businesses may survive well in the short term without good peripheral vision, but they become increasingly vulnerable and their position could be quickly eroded by something unexpected on their fringes. Given this lack of short-term demand from the immediate environment, the role of leadership becomes a crucial counterweight. Managers and leaders must make a conscious effort to develop and encourage these important capabilities from within.

In the following discussions, we consider each of these five components, how they relate to Mattel's story, and how they can be further honed as organizational meta-capabilities.

## Vigilant Leadership That Encourages a Broad Focus on the Periphery

A leader with strong peripheral vision can take the entire organization in new directions. For example, Comcast's Brian Roberts has not only moved the company out of a more limited geographic area but also shifted its focus beyond channels to content. Roberts's geographic expansion, including the acquisition of AT&T's cable business, built the company into the largest cable television operator in the United States. In a digital world with intense competition for communications channels, the company moved into areas that were initially considered peripheral. Comcast made a failed bid for the movies, sports, and other programs of Walt Disney Company and then joined with Sony in acquiring Metro-Goldwyn-Mayer's extensive film library. In 2004, Comcast spent over $4.5 billion on content in support of its on-demand strategy. This shift in focus, offering users access to hundreds of movies per month, was designed to differentiate the company from satellite and other competitors fighting for control of the digital pathways into the home.[8] All this strategic repositioning called for leadership that was willing and could look beyond the current business in cable service to more peripheral areas.

An astute investment manager with a successful twenty-five-year track record reflected on how he chose the small number of companies on which to bet. He concluded, as we found in our own research, that leadership was the cornerstone: "It all starts with the CEO. I've seen a lot of them, and the best ones are highly attuned to their periphery. As a result, their organizations can better see possibilities sooner . . . those that are tightly focused on the existing operations are good COOs. But they are not leaders for the long haul."

He noted that the best senior executives he had worked with all were strong conceptual thinkers who could foresee new patterns in their macro-environment. For example, he cited one CEO who pushed his organization to think through the implications of China hosting the Olympics, just after the announcement was made: "He didn't want just the obvious first-order effects concerning demand for construction products, but especially second-order effects on substitute products if prices were to rise."

As he thought further, the investment manager realized that the successful CEOs were all smart and secure and that they had no hesitation in surrounding themselves with strong people. They encouraged vigorous debate and dialogue because they didn't pretend to have all the answers. Their listening skills were complemented by a capacity to absorb a lot of information and deal with uncertainty. He summed up by observing, "If you only follow the conventional and direct implications, you'll just be part of the crowd—success comes from thinking more imaginatively." His long track record of remarkable wealth creation and his hard-earned insights about effective CEOs accords well with our own research.

In contrast, Mattel's leadership had narrowed its focus before the Bratz invasion due to an internal crisis. After Mattel's disastrous 1999 acquisition of educational software maker The Learning Company, which cost $3.8 billion and led the company to its first loss in more than a decade, CEO Robert Eckert was brought in from Kraft in May 2000 to turn the company around. He worked intently on various initiatives "to bring stability and predictability" to the company.[9]

This type of crisis tends to concentrate attention, reduce peripheral vision, and create a culture focused on short-term performance (performance organization) rather than longer-term and wider exploration (learning organization). While Mattel's cost cutting increased its profit margins, its gross U.S. sales declined by 11 percent in 2003, with Barbie's U.S. sales alone falling by 15 percent.[10] The company became increasingly efficient in a business with a shrinking share of the market. A broader scope, including competitive intelligence about changes in not only toys but video games, music, movies, and other forms of entertainment might have helped Mattel identify shifts in the market sooner.

Any organization needs the appropriate guidance and support from its leaders if it wishes to improve its peripheral vision. Since the periphery has few champions, it is by its very nature a murky, high-risk area. Few soldiers will scout there unless the senior command clearly endorses and rewards such excursions. Leadership is, above all, about taking the long view, rising above partisan concerns, and having the courage to take risks that could lose the leaders their jobs. Few managers are secure enough to adopt this posture.

While strong peripheral vision at the top of the organization is vital, leadership is needed at all other levels. Although we mostly think of leadership as flowing from the top down, Michael Useem and others have emphasized the importance of "leading up" as well.[11] Such leadership is particularly important when it comes to the periphery because employees deeper down in the organization may have the most original perspectives or deepest insights into changes at the periphery. They may be closer to the customer or the competition and may better appreciate changes in the channel mix. But their insight must receive a fair hearing for the organization to benefit. Effective leadership requires both the will to take the organization in new directions and the humility to listen to challenging perspectives from the periphery. James Collins has characterized this paradoxical combination of resolve and humility as "level 5 leadership" in his book *Good to Great*.[12]

## An Inquisitive Approach to Strategy Development

After the peripheral vision of the leader, the second component of a company's capability for peripheral vision is an inquisitive approach to strategic thinking and planning. An organization with strong peripheral vision tends to have a more flexible strategy process, with longer time horizons, incorporating diverse inputs and employing tools such as scenario planning, real-options thinking, and dynamic monitoring.

In contrast to the rigid budget-oriented planning in most organizations, which tends to keep managers focused on the current time period, market, and business, planning that strengthens peripheral vision should be flexible, issues-oriented, and farsighted. Managers should be encouraged to rethink their assumptions about plans and goals without penalty. Questions about strategy need to be shared broadly and debated throughout the organization. The strategy-making process also should incorporate diverse inputs, including insights about and from customers, competitive information, views of outside experts, and fresh thinking about new technologies that might disrupt the business.

Johnson & Johnson created a strategy process, called Frame-workS, to scan the volatile periphery. The company operates in a world that is complex and fast changing. Managers need to pay attention not only to markets and shifting technology but also to changing healthcare regulations, insurance coverage, and formularies as well as competitive moves in businesses ranging from retail products such as Band-Aids and Tylenol to disposable contact lenses and ethical pharmaceuticals. Its decentralized structure, with more than two hundred relatively autonomous operating companies around the world, helps keep its businesses close to the needs of their respective markets. But the company has also created a planning process that keeps an eye on the periphery.

As part of its FrameworkS process, the Executive Committee and members of the strategy task force ask themselves, What will the demographic picture be in 2010? What might the customer profiles look like in twenty years? How will a typical doctor's office or hospital operate? What role will government play? What will technology look like in 2010? What will be the role and power of the payers? These questions encourage a deep curiosity about the periphery.

To enhance peripheral vision, strategy making must balance question- or hypothesis-driven inquiry with an open, inquisitive mind that will pick up the unexpected. The Johnson & Johnson questions may lead the organization to consider radically different scenarios and new opportunities. But to do this well requires a high tolerance for ambiguity and even a willingness to embrace paradox.

As discussed in chapters 2 and 5, scenario planning and other future-mapping techniques can especially help to broaden strategic thinking and planning because they encourage diverse perspectives and keeping the process open to multiple interpretations. Other strategic capabilities such as experience in using real options (discussed in chapter 5) and the ability to build alliances can increase the organization's peripheral vision capacity. Alliance partners are often a valuable source of information about the periphery, contributing directly to organizational learning. But to capture this learning, the organization needs to have the capacity to manage the knowledge and insights generated from the partnership.[14]

Mattel's planning, in contrast, was primarily focused on its current line of products. Every year, Mattel came up with some 150 different Barbie dolls and 120 new outfits to keep Barbie on the cutting edge of fashion. But this emphasis on incremental improvements within the brand drew attention away from its seeing the age compression among its target customer segments. Focus groups with current customers to refine the Barbie line could not identify the shifts in the customer base or the defection of older girls who no longer saw Barbie as attractive or relevant. With a wider scope, Mattel might have applied different scanning tools to look more broadly at the periphery. It could have looked more closely at defectors and dissatisfied customers. The organization could have tried approaches such as Nike and Reebok's use of cool hunters to find trendsetters outside the current customer base. Mattel also might have provided incentives to employees and retailers to provide fresh information about changes in the market.

## A Flexible and Inquisitive Culture

Because not all of these processes can be finely orchestrated, measured numerically, or rewarded monetarily, the third component of a capability for peripheral vision is a culture and norms that encourage appropriate behavior. Cultures tend to change very slowly, usually in response to success in changing the other capabilities related to peripheral vision. Many corporate cultures are risk averse and conservative, with limited flexibility to scope and scan widely. Consequently, the likelihood that they will fail to see relevant data outside their focal vision increases. An organization's culture, however, can provide a counterweight by encouraging curiosity that leads to better peripheral vision.

Blogs (which we discussed as a source of broad insights in chapter 3) can be an effective mechanism for encouraging organizational curiosity. For example, Sun Microsystems encourages all of its thirty-two thousand employees to create online blogs. Although only about a hundred are actively doing so, they include President and COO Jonathan Schwartz, who writes a blog that is read by some thirty-five thousand employees, customers, partners, and even competitors. He uses the blog to share his insights on changes in technology and the industry. While Schwartz says the blogs are not mandatory in the company, any more than e-mail use is mandatory, he adds, "I have a hard time seeing how a manager can be effective without both."

Too often, however, an organizational culture limits its peripheral vision. The culture at the *New York Times* under the leadership of executive editor Howell Raines was shaped by an executive described as "an ego-driven autocrat who ruled by fear . . . and loathed hearing unwanted truth."[14] While Raines's single-minded focus helped the newspaper to win a record of seven Pulitzer Prizes in one year, the limits of the culture contributed to the scandal surrounding the plagiarism and fabrications of reporter Jayson Blair. The increasingly strong messages from the periphery that there were problems with Blair's reporting were dismissed by Raines, who resigned when the scandal broke in June 2003. Similarly, the powerful but reckless culture of Enron, encouraged by a board that looked the other way, allowed scandals to unfold that ultimately brought about the company's demise.

Companies in some industries have cultures more focused on the periphery. Firms in the fashion industry or those dealing with fickle consumer markets, for example, are often compelled to develop strong peripheral vision merely to survive in such dynamic environments.[15] Other organizations have strengths in knowledge management and inquiring systems.[16] These organizations can offer models and approaches that can be emulated.

Mattel had very much a product-driven culture at the time Bratz was launched. Its internal focus was evident in the one-hundred-plus-page manual governing all the "dos and don'ts" of handling the Barbie brand. Because the company was a market leader, it adopted a defensive posture, tweaking the product line and making small improvements rather than truly trying to understand the evolving needs of its target customers and beyond.

*Create an Ecology of Warning to Move Information Across the Organization*  This culture could be designed to create what the CIA refers to as an *ecology of warning*. The goal is to encourage people to pay attention to warning signals, even if they are not related to their current task. For example, a firefighter who goes into the home of an elderly person might be given training and incentives to recognize that the clutter in the house increases the risk of a hip fracture. The firefighter would then alert the person's caregivers or HMO to take steps to prevent such an accident. There might also be prizes or bulletin boards to celebrate such actions. Normally, the firefighter would just focus on responding to the fire call, but with an ecology of warning the firefighter helps to prevent future accidents. Organizations, likewise, need to look for ways to encourage their existing networks of sensors to share information about early signals that might be important to other parts of the organization. This ecology of warning can be encouraged through incentives and training, as discussed next.

## Knowledge Systems for Detecting and Sharing Weak Signals

A British supermarket noticed that sales of its expensive French cheeses had declined. But before it pulled them from its cases, it cross-checked this information with its customer database. Thanks to customer loyalty cards, this retailer had extensive knowledge about the purchasing patterns of its customers. The database revealed that, while the sales of French cheeses were relatively small, they were being purchased by the supermarket's most profitable customers. The company kept the cheeses in its stores.[17]

While this example demonstrates the payoffs from systems that gather and mine customer information, it also shows their limitations. For example, what other products, like French cheeses, could be added to bring in new profitable customers who have never walked into the store? What larger trends in society are behind the interest in French cheeses, and how can the company capitalize on them? Are other competitors taking advantage of this and other trends, such as more sophisticated tastes, ready-to-eat meals, or organic produce? Loyalty cards and other systems for gathering customer information offer a detailed, but only partial, picture of current customers; there is a much bigger world out there. Reading the weak signals of current customers and competitors is a good first step, but seeing and interpreting the messy weak signals from the broader world is a much bigger challenge.

Organizations with good peripheral vision possess strong capabilities in knowledge systems, particularly the identification of weak signals from the avalanche of data in our digital world. And they know how to share this information across organizational boundaries. Due to data mining, companies have built Everests of data that have often turned out to be insurmountable; companies have become data rich and synthesis poor. British retailer Safeway, for example, eliminated its customer loyalty cards after realizing that it didn't have the capacity to use the data they were generating. In addition to customer and competitor information, vast amounts of data are generated within the company, such as insights from individual sales representatives.

William Gibson once said, "The future is here. It's just not widely distributed yet." Organizations need to create channels for distributing the knowledge and insights about the future that are already present in the organization. As discussed in chapter 3, companies need to scan for information inside the firm. Increasingly, organizations are trying to draw together information sources into easily accessible knowledge management systems. And, of course, there is the wild and seemingly boundless expanse of the World Wide Web. Companies are beginning to focus their "Hubble telescopes" on this vast, unstructured, and unreliable universe to glean specific insights. How to manage this avalanche of data lies at the heart of the information-sharing capability.

Managers should consider whether there are significant *structural holes* in their information systems, areas that should be receiving information but aren't because of the social networks at play.[18] If there are, they can try to close these holes through improving organizational systems for making sense. Similarly, managers might ask if their organization suffers from *black holes*, areas in the organization that are sinkholes for information. Akin to black holes in astrophysics, these are clusters (i.e., groups, departments, or functions) from which no light or information ever emanates; these units suck in a lot of information but seldom share it. When weak signals encounter black holes along their convoluted path from faint stirring to meaningful information, they may be stopped dead in their tracks. And if certain parts of the organization are too isolated from knowledgeable others, they can become structural holes that fail to recognize, enhance, and act on peripheral information relevant to the enterprise overall.

Mattel's missteps against Bratz were not due to lack of data. The company collects extensive data about sales; receives marketing research from no less than five companies; and sets up focus groups, mall intercepts, and even visits to children's homes to understand changing patterns of play. It had seen the first signs of age compression all the way back in the 1980s. But its information systems in 2000 consisted of two hundred fragmented enterprise systems that didn't easily share data because most were custom built. In a conference call with analysts in 2002, the new CIO Joseph Eckroth said that these systems hindered productivity, reduced operating efficiency, and slowed the company's ability to react to changes in its environment. Early in 2002, Mattel launched an overhaul of its information system. But, perhaps distracted by its financial challenges, the company failed to "connect the dots" and respond quickly to what it saw. With its decades of investments in Barbie, Mattel also had much more to lose, which resulted in a much more cautious attitude. When it launched its Diva Starz line, with a bit hipper fashion, it ran into customer opposition. Besides, Barbie was still growing when Bratz arrived, and the doll had brushed aside earlier threats. A Little Mermaid doll that had achieved success, for example, was pushed back into the sea by a Barbie with a fish tail.[19] Companies that have ruled their markets for years are especially at risk for overlooking peripheral forces that change the familiar landscape.

Mattel's organizational structure also didn't help internal communications. Prior to the formation of Mattel Brands in 2003, the boys' and girls' divisions of Mattel operated like an independent fraternity and sorority, respectively. (Even before their much publicized "breakup," Barbie and Ken did not often speak with each other.) There was little interaction among these divisions and little career movement across the company's different brands. The new Mattel Brands structure instituted in 2003 was designed to create more interaction across the boys and girls organizations, but by then Bratz was already firmly entrenched.

*Eliminate or Challenge the Silos.* Organizational stovepipes can impede or facilitate sharing information. For example, while the decentralized marketing responsibilities of Starbucks ensured that managers were attuned to local tastes, it also became harder for the central organization to recognize broader changes. While the company was considered one of the most astute marketing organizations in the world, it had no strategic marketing group or chief marketing officer. Marketing responsibilities were spread across three separate groups (market research, category, and marketing groups). In 2002, this hampered the company's recognition that its brand was weakening; that its changing customer base was shifting toward younger, less-well-educated and lower-income consumers; and that customer satisfaction was declining. The information about these trends was available in individual stores, but due to a weakness in organizational configuration, these insights were not drawn together rapidly. The big-picture insights were only slowly recognized.[20] Companies can expand the frame of managers by reshaping stovepipes or creating integrating structures around them.

*Capture Faint Stirrings.* The capacity for managing consumer data is continually improving. Companies are using real-time information to adjust prices, for example. They are adding predictive analytics that help anticipate where the trends are headed. But these two advances are primarily concerned with structured data about the current business, which falls mostly within the focal vision of the organization. The challenge is to deal with messy, unstructured data as well. Organizations must give appropriate attention to the outliers and weak signals that are often filtered out in systems looking for definitive insights.

The discipline of knowledge management has emerged to help with the overload of information, building on traditional archival approaches and more modern decision-support methodologies. The challenge in all these systems is to decide what is deserving of storage before we know its true relevance and how to retrieve it later when needed. This is an especially daunting task for peripheral information, which tends to be incomplete, ambiguous, and seemingly of low relevance. To store all faint stirrings would be foolish, but to filter tightly may sift out important signals.

One way to identify significant threats is to designate one executive to "collect the paranoia." That person should be senior enough to gain a hearing in the organization, ensuring that the negative, life-threatening information will be taken seriously. Another approach for capturing and acting on faint stirrings is to mount search parties of two or three people from different departments. These groups should consider the question: What is the worst thing that could happen to our new product line this year? Once these threats are identified, the group can draw up a list of warning signs. After looking at the potential for disaster, the group can also consider what is the best thing that could happen to the company. This will make the organization more attentive to the faint stirrings and allow managers to more quickly "connect the dots."

*Use Market Mechanisms and Advanced Analytics to See the Big Picture.* A former CIA director proposed designing a market for terrorism, so that government officials as well as the public could monitor how well-informed players assess the chances of various terrorist acts occurring (such as the destruction of the Eiffel Tower in Paris or Big Ben in London). Political opposition to betting on terror and misfortune quickly squelched this idea, even though the notion of expert panels and opinion markets has much to recommend itself. Academic research has amply demonstrated the wisdom of markets or crowds.[21] Such artificial shadow markets can be designed to track and reward superior insights on any topic. For example, there exists a very accurate market for predicting presidential elections where people vote with their money and reputations.

The key is to design a constellation of specialized as well as general-purpose intelligence-gathering devices that monitor the periphery in much the same way that military intelligence scans the surface of the globe and the skies above for unusual occurrences. Managers can increasingly avail themselves of powerful information-processing technologies for the detection, codification, storage, transmission, and even interpretation of data. While most executive dashboards tend to narrow the focus of the business, broader systems can be designed to track key developments in the periphery and expert panels can be remotely convened to render verdicts about ambiguous information. IBM's WebFountain (discussed in chapter 3) is perhaps the most ambitious, systematic attempt in the private sector to codify the periphery by constantly drawing in data from cyberspace and other sources. Technologies, from pattern recognition to information storage and retrieval to encryption, continue to advance the ability of organizations to peer into the periphery.

## Develop an Organizational Configuration and Processes That Encourage the Exploration of the Periphery

Leadership, strategic planning processes, culture, and knowledge-sharing systems that encourage peripheral vision need to be supported by an appropriate organizational architecture. After the Bratz attack on Barbie, Mattel launched a center of innovation, dubbed Project Platypus, that brings diverse teams together to create new product ideas. It is designed to develop new hit products rather than the next iteration of Barbie or me-too responses to Bratz. The dozen members of the project rotate out of their regular duties to take three-month stints at a studio that is designed for play and creativity. They form teams that go out on field trips to watch children play, interview parents, and creatively brainstorm to create new product concepts.[22] People align around ideas that they are passionate about. This initiative is not just creating ideas for projects and market innovations. Through the steady rotation of new participants, it is also diffusing its approaches to creativity throughout the larger organization.

This type of initiative has helped the company create truly new products such as Ello, an original "creation system" targeted toward girls five to ten years old, which can be used to build everything from houses to people to necklaces. Ello helped to drive up sales of Mattel's Other Girls Brands by 5 percent globally in 2003. By establishing Project Platypus, the company, in essence, created new rod cells to detect opportunities on the periphery sooner and reconfigured the organization to allow these insights to grow into new products. Similarly, Procter & Gamble established a system that takes managers out of their jobs temporarily and challenges them to create a rapid-prototyping plan for a significant new business in a very short period of time (see box, "Discontinuity Boot Camp"). Such initiatives can shake up and expand the narrow focus of managers.

Other organizational structures can also contribute to peripheral vision. As discussed in chapter 5, the CIA created an external venture fund, In-Q-Tel, to find and assess emerging technologies that could be useful to it. Companies have created investment funds, such as Intel Capital, whose aim is to keep a close eye on emerging technologies. Other key aspects of the internal organizational configuration that can help strengthen peripheral insights include hiring employees who expand the curiosity and diversity of perspectives of the organization and creating incentives to encourage and reward peripheral vision among individuals. Assigning clear accountability for the periphery is important, as we discuss in the following chapter.

*Hire, Train, and Reward for Curiosity.* Some people have a greater innate ability to scan the periphery than others. When you attend a party or reception, how much do you notice about the periphery? Who is talking to whom, who leaves early, and where does there seem to be laughter or tension? Some individuals notice everything that happens, while others leave noticing little, even about the few people they have spoken with during the evening. To enhance organizational curiosity, the human resource function—which deals

# Discontinuity Boot Camp

Procter & Gamble created an approach called Discontinuity Boot Camp, a name that sent a clear signal that the work was expected to challenge the status quo. During the boot camp, managers are taken offsite and challenged to create an original product idea in a very short period of time. Whereas innovators once had to scribble their ideas on the backs of napkins, technology now helps in the process of prototyping new ideas. The use of simulations provides information acceleration and aids the creation of rough video prototypes that describe the proposed concept. A prototype television advertisement can quickly make an unimaginable idea much more real and clarify its potential in a very visceral way. This approach gives the managers involved and those evaluating the concept the opportunity to assess whether the appeal of the concept is strong enough and differentiated enough to warrant the time and resources needed to develop it more fully. Evaluators of these new ideas can also look at something they can't find in a standard business plan, a sense of passion and excitement about the idea. Is this a business with power?

This whole process is much faster and rougher than the way things are typically done. When exploring the periphery, the goal is not to see in everything in great detail but to determine quickly whether the object is worthy of more organizational attention. These approaches, in essence, allow the organization to take a quick side glance at something to determine whether to turn more attention to this concept on the fringes.[a]

a. Larry Huston, "Mining the Periphery for New Products," *Long Range Planning* 37 (2004), 191–196.

with recruitment, training, promotion, and compensation—can be an important lever in changing the composition of individuals who make up the organization.

Organizations can design for diversity across the workforce and for strong individual peripheral vision among new hires, both of which can contribute to organizational scanning. When hiring new staff, specific questions can be posed or tests administered to assess a person's interest and ability to scan the periphery without taking his or her eye off the ball. When designing performance reviews, evaluate how frequently and successfully items from the periphery were noticed. And in training programs, include workshops on critical and innovative thinking, scenario planning, dynamic monitoring, and weak-signal detection. Educate your employees about the cognitive filters and biases we all, at times, fall victim to as we try to make sense of the outside world.

## Conclusion: Putting It All Together

The components that make up an organization's capability for peripheral vision are highly interlinked, as illustrated in figure 7-2. They should all reinforce one another, with leadership as the overarching theme. Strong leadership can do a lot to make the periphery real throughout the organization.

Sometimes, however, the interrelationships are complex or subtle. A strength in one area, which appears to improve peripheral vision, may actually decrease peripheral vision by limiting flexibility and curiosity. For example, Cisco's ability to close its books in real time through a "virtual close" made it seem highly attuned to the environment. Instead of waiting for a month to know how its businesses were doing, it could know where it stood from day to day, putting its finger on the financial pulse of its business. While this

FIGURE 7-2

## Components of peripheral vision capability

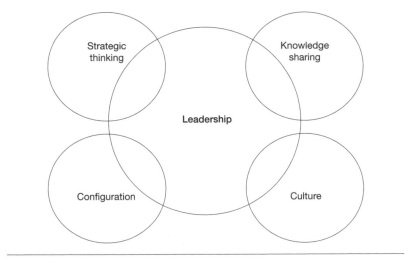

focused its attention on the current business in real time, it didn't necessarily help the company recognize the broader changes in the environment that ultimately affected the business. The company was slow to spot the recession that followed the dot-com collapse, forcing Cisco to take an inventory charge of billions of dollars in 2001. Perhaps this couldn't have been avoided, but closing its books in real time gave the company a very accurate rear-view mirror, not a better view of the road ahead. Indeed, such real-time management systems may create a false sense of security.

Whereas each of the recommendations in this chapter by itself can improve peripheral vision, an integrated approach will provide far more power. When designing inquisitive organizations, managers are well advised to adopt a systems view in which the total is more than the sum of its parts. Various internal organizational forces will seek to maintain the status quo and oppose any source of change. The rubber-band theory applies. An isolated small change is like pulling a rubber band slightly and then letting it go. The rubber band will quickly snap back to its original state, and so will the organization if the change effort is not supported by reinforcing changes. Each of the recommendations given here can reinforce the others. But companies have to strike the right balance between resources allocated to their peripheral versus their focal vision. In the following chapter, we provide further insights on assessing and improving peripheral vision in your own organization, especially in the role of the leader.

# Chapter Eight

# Leading

## An Agenda for Action

*"Giving up the illusion that you can predict the future is a very liberating moment. All you can do is to give yourself the capacity to respond to the only certainty in life—which is uncertainty. The creation of that capability is the purpose of strategy."*

—*Lord John Browne, Group Chief Executive of BP*[1]

A S AN EXECUTIVE of the BBC flew out of London, she looked down at the futuristic contours of the controversial Millennium Dome along the Thames. She reflected that her organization must balance the slow-moving traditions that meander like this river with the challenges of a digital world that rises with all the hype and uncertain promise of the sweeping white dome. As she lifted above this complex landscape of the city and the BBC, she wondered, How can we lead the way into this new world and remain relevant to the audiences who pay for it?

The BBC, Britain's publicly funded, public-service broadcasting service, was facing a complex set of challenges. Throughout 2004, the BBC looked as if it was in deep trouble.[2] Two of its top officers resigned after a rancorous investigation of an inaccurate allegation about the "fixing" of Iraq war intelligence. There also were widespread criticisms of the license fee—a compulsory tax levied on the 24 million U.K. households with a television set (although it pays for U.K. national and regional TV, radio, online, and interactive services). And technology continued to change. As digital broadcasting enabled more than four hundred channels—compared with four as recently as the early 1980s—the BBC's competitors had become even more irate at the way it was being financed. In 2005, in this hectic climate, the BBC was negotiating its charter, which authorizes the service's very existence and the collection of the license fees that generate the bulk of its £3 billion ($5.6 billion) operating revenue. This revenue supports the BBC's eight television channels, ten radio networks, and acclaimed online service across the United Kingdom and the Commonwealth. Additional revenue is generated through two commercial divisions—BBC Worldwide Ltd. and BBC Ventures Group Ltd.—that sell goods and services around the world.

The programming of the BBC is a constant experiment, and the tastes of the public are often hard to predict. For example, in 2005 the BBC's classical station, Radio 3, spent an entire week playing every piece Beethoven ever wrote, along with supporting dramas and documentaries on television. It was a huge success. There were 620,000 downloads of the five symphonies on the first five days of the broadcast (and 1.4 million at the end of all nine symphonies), which would have put the composer at positions 1–5 on the download charts—ahead of the hot pop bands.

But one of the most important shifts was the digital revolution, with a proliferation of devices and content available on a wide range of digital platforms. By 2005, broadcasts were already available via digital television, the Internet, and mobile devices. Listeners could also receive thousands of international stations. These technology trends aided and abetted the fragmentation of the audience and helped to accelerate changes in viewing and listening tastes. The organization needed to balance R&D and new media with fulfilling its core creative, democratic, social, and cultural purposes. How could the BBC act on this broad and shifting periphery without becoming neurotic and distracted?

## Mining or Minding the Periphery

The BBC faces a very broad and ambiguous set of threats and challenges at its periphery. It must "mind" a broad periphery and act to understand and capitalize on relevant changes, particularly in distribution and audience consumption habits.[3] This requires *divergent* attention and actions across many areas. In contrast, when dealing with a well-defined part of the periphery, such as the threat of LEDs to the lighting industry (discussed in chapter 6), leaders can encourage the organization to "mine" in a specific area. Mining requires a more *convergent* focus on a specific part of the periphery and requires rapidly developing the capacity to respond to it. (Of course, there may be other shifts beyond LEDs that the managers in the lighting industry should mind more broadly. For example, what will be the cumulative impact of the mercury pollution associated with traditional lightbulbs?)

The danger for an organization that seeks to mind a broad periphery is that this attention may become too diffuse. The BBC avoided this by encouraging the organization to mind the periphery in certain ways—it mobilized the organization to be more inquisitive, directed attention to specific challenges, and broadly tracked various trends and tastes. There were other dimensions to the minding strategy, but let's examine these three in greater detail to better appreciate the approach.

### Mobilize the Organization to Become More Inquisitive

When new BBC General-Director Mark Thompson was appointed in June 2004, he set about passionately focusing organizational attention on how the outside world was changing. He had walked into a small consumer electronics store and seen an HDTV camera for a very low price. The BBC was still talking about HDTV. The consumer was already using it. The future is here, he thought, and the BBC needed to better understand it. He announced a restructuring of the executive committee and set in motion a review that challenged business operations. While the organization needed to cut costs, he made it clear that the bigger focus should be on asking questions that would challenge the way its members thought about their business. As he told the twenty-eight thousand BBC staff members around the United Kingdom on his first day, "We are going into this with a genuinely open mind but these are questions which are not going to go away. If we did not examine them thoroughly ourselves, others would do it for us . . . Our task is going to be to change the BBC more rapidly and radically over the next three to five years than at any previous point in its history."[4]

Because the organization has such a broad periphery, it was important that he didn't provide employees with simple answers. Instead, he challenged the organization to better understand diverse aspects of the periphery. Thompson launched an initiative called Creative Future to encourage every part of the organization to focus on paying attention to the changes that would define their future.

The goal was to get everyone in the organization looking outside at the periphery—particularly at new technology, channels, and consumer behavior—to better understand how his or her own part of the business might change. It was a culture change, from focusing narrowly on delivering news and other broadcasts to looking much more broadly. It encouraged the entire organization to engage in scanning, sharing information, and creating organizational space to discuss what these signals might mean.

This culture change prompted diverse insights and actions in different parts of the organization. For example, in seeking to understand younger audiences, BBC's marketers discovered that, while young viewers liked specific BBC programs, they did not associate the programs with the overall brand. The BBC then devised corporate image-building campaigns to raise awareness and shift perceptions that the programming these viewers liked so much actually came from the BBC. The challenge was to reach this younger audience on their own turf and in their own language.

## Focus Attention on Specific Challenges

The problem with a broad periphery is that the organization can easily become overwhelmed and its attention can become diffuse. There is a vital need for prioritization and focus to direct attention to specific areas while continuing to promote a broad awareness. In discussing peripheral vision, Procter & Gamble executive Larry Huston recalled how he was taught as a child to look for Native American arrowheads and other artifacts in farmers' plowed fields in eastern Pennsylvania. An undirected search was rarely successful, so Huston was taught by his father to search using a stick, randomly poking the point of the stick into the field and focusing his eyes only at the end of the stick. Although this search was random, the point of the stick focused his attention on an area sufficiently narrow to see small artifacts that would have been lost in a wider gauge..

At the BBC, Thompson created specific initiatives to focus organizational attention on understanding in detail the changes in the landscape. These initiatives were not quite as random as Huston's stick, but they served the similar purpose of directing attention to narrower, significant areas of the periphery. Digital technology was one of these areas of focus. (And while it started as a relatively small area of attention, it is now receiving tremendous attention within and outside the BBC.) A week after his arrival, Thompson and BBC Chairman Michael Grade released a nine-point manifesto as part of the Charter Renewal campaign for changing the organization to meet the demands and opportunities of a digital age. They envisioned a world in which everyone in the United Kingdom has equal access to digital services—on demand, portable, and personalized—in which "the traditional one-way traffic from broadcaster to consumer evolves into a true creative dialogue in which the public are not passive audiences but active, inspired participants."[5] The document created a context for the organization to heed the implications of these technologies and to move on opportunities of the digital world.

The BBC also worked with outside consultants to examine some of the changes in the outside world and achieve needed cultural changes within the organization. This made the company realize that its audience was far ahead of the BBC in adopting new technologies such as digital video recorders, wikis, and text messaging on cell phones. How, where, and why consumers access media and entertainment had changed dramatically.

The BBC has conducted a variety of experiments to respond to profoundly different audience behaviors, such as downloading, interacting, manipulating, and co-creating content. The broadcast company developed a radio player that allows extended Web access to on-air content. This, in turn, led to an Interactive Media Player and a MyBBC Player that allows license payers to search and access the BBC archive. All these initiatives constitute real-world tests of the periphery.

## Actively Track Trends and Tastes

The BBC also tapped into trend-spotting cool hunters to scan, search, and feed in to the creative production process. It also looked at precursors. Their chief technology officer (CTO) is a frequent visitor to South Korea and other parts of Asia that are precursors to the type of digital world the BBC is developing in the West. The CTO is looking specifically for insights into the BBC's own business: What impact can the new technology have on the way consumers gather news, entertainment, and information? What are the most important channels when news and entertainment are consumed via cell phones, computer, and television? What about Podcasts? Which types of content work best through which distribution channels? (For example, they are creating "mobisodes," short extracts of large shows sent straight to mobile phones.) How can the experience in the United Kingdom be expected to be similar or different?

The BBC also looked at changes in society at home, which led to unexpected insights. One of the key trends it recognized, for example, was that more people live alone. This leads to less family viewing and far more individual viewing. Even in households with many members, the purchase of multiple televisions means that people are living in their own "information cocoon," so there are fewer opportunities for shared experiences. This insight created opportunities for new programming that can draw families together around one television screen. For example, BBC relaunched *Dr. Who*, which has been wildly successful in a typical dead-zone program time on Saturday at 7 p.m., in large part because the program can draw together the entire family. It surprised the whole industry that Saturday night wasn't dead, and even in an age of fragmenting media, there was a market for more traditional entertainment that can draw people together.

Blogging is also changing the BBC's relationship with its audiences in the United Kingdom and around the world. Citizen journalism is an important new development, where tourists photograph and share pictures of tsunamis or bombings, bloggers update the news, and interactive media are gaining power. Such technology-driven developments are clearly changing the BBC's interactions with its audience. And these changes also raise serious challenges about ensuring that the BBC's core values of integrity, impartiality, and trust are consistent and sustained in this new "wiki" world.

These are just a few examples of how the BBC tried to mind its rather broad periphery. In practice, the distinction between minding and mining the periphery is a matter of degree. Every organization must watch smaller areas of interest and not lose sight of the big picture.

## Six Lessons from the Periphery

What are the guiding principles for leaders, such as the BBC's Mark Thompson, who must lead their organizations into the periphery? We have extracted a set of core lessons from our discussions on the preceding pages that can help organizations and individual managers get a better handle on the periphery without becoming overloaded and confused:

*Lesson 1: Peripheral vision is more about anticipation and alertness than prediction.*[6] One of the overriding principles of effective peripheral vision is that it will always be less clear than focal vision. The periphery is blurry; it is not in color. Weak signals are by definition faint. The future is basically unknowable. Even with these limitations, however, peripheral vision enables two kinds of anticipation: preparing in the face of uncertainty and acting before anyone else can. By the time a clear prediction or forecast can be made, it is probably too late. Organizations monitoring the periphery can position themselves shrewdly. While we have a deep human desire for certainty and precision, we must become comfortable with a world that is blurry if we are ever to see beyond the bounds of our focal vision.

*Lesson 2: The problem is not a lack of data but a lack of good questions.* Managers console themselves by gathering more information, but unless they focus this gathering on expanding the field of vision, no matter how carefully they look, they won't see opportunities and threats unless their scope is broad enough. The right guiding questions will direct the attention of the entire organization to the places that matter while filtering out the meaningless noise.

*Lesson 3: Scan actively but with an open mind because the periphery won't always come to you.* Don't wait for the periphery to come to you; often, you must explore it. Columbus didn't reach America merely by staring out to sea; he set sail. While passive scanning plays an important role in peripheral vision, you also must explore the periphery actively through directed hypotheses and undirected journeys into the unknown. In particular, you can use various tools to focus attention on specific parts of the periphery—such as customer shifts or emerging technologies—that are particularly important to your firm or the question under consideration. Active scanning is not a one-time or annual event. It must be a real-time process that draws on a broad repertoire of techniques and approaches.

*Lesson 4: Use triangulation to better understand the periphery.* Just as the eye uses triangulation to provide depth and meaning, multiple perspectives on the periphery are needed to comprehend it. If the periphery is confusing, look at it from different angles. This is most easily done by bringing different people with diverse views into the process and by using multiple methods or techniques. This is especially important because the periphery is inherently blurry and incomplete. The conflicts and differences in viewpoints, as well as multiple hypotheses, can help illuminate different parts of the picture. In this way, the organization can think creatively to "connect the dots."

*Lesson 5: When catching glimpses from the periphery, it is wise to probe before jumping.* Don't always trust what you see out of the corner of your eye. It is important not to jump to conclusions but to take time to learn more about the periphery. We must amplify the weak signals with directed probes. We also must act prudently through a portfolio of real options and experiments to maintain flexibility until the uncertainty is more tolerable.[7]

*Lesson 6: Balancing peripheral and focal vision is a central leadership challenge.* The resources and attention devoted to the periphery are often taken away from investments in the focal area. Organizations must strike the right balance between focal and peripheral vision. The eye works its wondrous way by combining inputs from the rod cells that are scanning the periphery and the cone cells that are used for focal vision in good lighting conditions. Both rods and cones have their roles; in the same way, organizations must not view peripheral activities as a distraction or diversion of scarce resources that should be devoted to focal concerns. Leaders must strike the right balance based on the needs of the organization and its environment. Some will need a tightly focused organization, while others must develop a truly "ambidextrous" organization that can both manage small incremental moves and lead revolutionary changes.

## Agenda for Improvement

If the organization has weaknesses in its peripheral vision, it must develop an agenda for improvement. Once these weaknesses are identified, there are many ways to address these deficiencies, just as there is a wide range of options for treating weaknesses in human peripheral vision (see box, "Treating Poor Peripheral Vision"). The preceding chapters offer specific strategies for the processes and capabilities that can strengthen an organization's peripheral vision.

### Check Your Vision

Just as the optometrist sends a reminder card for an annual check up, get into the habit of regularly assessing the peripheral vision of your organization using the Strategic Eye Exam (see appendix A). Has your environment changed in a way that is making peripheral vision more important? Are you making progress in

---

# Treating Poor Peripheral Vision

How are defects in peripheral vision treated? Among the treatments for diseases such as retinitis pigmentosa that reduce peripheral vision are (with their business parallels noted in parentheses):

- Transplanting good retinal cells from donors (hiring individual employees or consultants to offer new insights)

- Transplanting whole eyes (bringing in a new CEO or initiating a substantial restructuring to change perspectives)

- Using stem cells to encourage the growth of ocular tissue (creating internal educational programs and initiatives to build broader perspectives in the existing organization)

- Using electronic or artificial aids (using technology to augment, amplify, and organize information from the environment to challenge existing perspectives)

---

building your organizational capabilities? Are you encountering fewer shocks and surprises or more of them? Use the exam with managers throughout the organization. The exam can, first of all, help to raise awareness of the importance of peripheral vision. Second, it can be a provocative discussion tool. We often find wide differences among members of a senior management team in their answers to specific questions because of differences in the way they scan, how broadly they scan, and how attuned they are to the periphery. By surfacing and challenging the different assumptions that are used—and making them explicit—the team becomes more responsive to the periphery. Third, the exam can serve as an educational or definitional tool, helping senior management teams to better understand the scope and complexity of their periphery.

As organizations recognize the importance of peripheral vision, they may want to make this kind of assessment more frequently than once or twice a year. They may ultimately replace their current dashboards with a broader strategic radar.[8] This radar could help to track the company's progress along current metrics but could also monitor the blips that may be moving in from the periphery. Such a radar could be used to recognize when a rival is launching an attack and to determine when gathering clouds are signs of passing showers or the warnings of a coming hurricane.

## Mind the Gap

The Strategic Eye Exam in appendix A will help you assess your own vigilance gap between your current capabilities for peripheral vision and your needs. Like athletes, organizations may be born with certain strengths and weaknesses in peripheral vision based on their history, structure, and industry. But they also can train and develop to improve this peripheral vision (perhaps more easily than athletes because the human body is a bit less malleable than an organization).

If the vigilance gap is great, the following strategic initiatives, taken from the preceding chapters, might help to narrow it:

- *Broaden or adjust the scope.* Review the strategic planning process to make it more outwardly oriented, including scanning the edges of business. In what ways does the current organization narrow the view of the world? Are there silos, filters, and blind spots in the organization? How can these be addressed to set the proper scope?

- *Strengthen scanning.* Determine how the company can scan different parts of the periphery more effectively. Can the organization create and develop a dynamic monitoring system that tracks external events, especially those that don't fit? Is there an opportunity to move from a corporate dashboard to a strategic radar that picks up weak signals?

- *Improve interpretation.* Look for ways to draw in additional insights to add depth to the picture. Integrate these different viewpoints inside and outside the organization into a coherent view of the world. The key is to triangulate using a variety of methods.

- *Actively probe.* Determine how the company can look more closely at interesting weak signals. How can you create options that allow the organization to explore weak signals without overcommitting?

- *Act wisely.* Based on the challenge at the periphery, match the company's actions to the level of uncertainty in the environment and competitive threats. Adopt a real-options mentality as you position for multiple futures.

- *Reconfigure the organization.* Vigilant organizations need leadership that encourages a broad focus on the periphery, an inquisitive approach to strategy making, a flexible and inquisitive culture that rewards exploring the edge, knowledge systems for detecting and sharing weak signals, and an organizational configuration and processes that encourage the exploration of the periphery. Among the areas that may need rethinking are incentive systems (do they encourage people to pick up and share weak signals?), channels for knowledge sharing, and hiring and promotion policies. Does the company tend to draw in employees who naturally have strong peripheral vision, or does its hiring and training reward employees with narrow expertise and limited attention spans? What is the right balance? If the gap is great, rethinking the organization is especially important. In particular, the improvement program should focus on the three most important levers that we found in our research: leadership, incentives, and a configuration that encourages the sharing of information.

- *Refocus leadership.* Above all, leadership is essential. Leaders should walk the talk, practicing leadership, demonstrating an interest in the periphery, and rewarding the peripheral insights of employees. Organizations should focus on mining specific areas of the periphery and minding broader areas of interest. The organization also can launch awareness-building and training programs to sensitize people to the periphery and introduce tools for peripheral vision more broadly. In addition to leadership with strong peripheral vision, the organization needs a board that is truly ambidextrous (i.e., good at dealing with the focal issues as well as the periphery). As with any change initiative, a sound improvement program has the following features:

1. Involves the entire organization from top to bottom

2. Focuses on the conditions enabling people to get good results

3. Recognizes that cultural change follows from behavioral change

4. Values deeds more than words[9]

Naturally, each organization will need a somewhat different action plan depending on the gap, its culture, resources, and other factors.

## Assign Accountability

Everyone in the organization may contribute to its peripheral vision, but if something is the responsibility of everyone, it often becomes the responsibility of no one. A central issue in configuring the organization is assigning accountability. Who in the organization is accountable for paying attention to the periphery? How should the organization design its "eyes" to look into the periphery? Among the possible configurations are these:

1. *Assign the responsibility to an existing functional group.* Groups such as corporate development, competitor intelligence, market research, or technology forecasting can be given the task of scanning. The risk is that these midlevel groups may limit their roles to narrowly collecting and processing data from the domain they know best rather than scanning broadly and educating others about what they have learned.

2. *Mobilize ad hoc issue groups.* The CEO or executive committee, along with the board, could identify the most pressing issues and then form separate task forces to pursue each issue. This process often is guided by a scenario analysis to identify key uncertainties to understand and monitor them better.

3. *Create a high-level lookout.* IBM has an ongoing capability called Crow's Nest that scans specific zones of the periphery and shares insights with top management. These zones

might include time compression, customer diversity, globalization, or networks. The responsibility of the group is to rise above functional and product blinders like a crow's nest on a ship, where lookouts watch for new land and dangerous reefs ahead.

4. *Create game-changing initiatives.* To push managers toward the periphery, Royal Dutch/Shell launched its GameChanger program in 1996. This program was designed to encourage managers to envision and test hypotheses about new opportunities beyond the core. In its first six years, the program screened four hundred ideas, commercialized more than thirty technologies, and created three new businesses.[10] Other companies, including New York Life Insurance, have launched similar initiatives, often with great results.

5. *Invest in start-up ventures.* Most large firms in the technology sector have a pool of capital to invest in promising start-ups, and this fund can be accountable for monitoring developments at the periphery. These investments may be modest but sufficient to get a clear view of the emerging technology and market. If the start-up succeeds, then an option to acquire can be exercised. Sony, for example, has a venture portfolio of around nine hundred companies.

6. *Outsource.* The company can also outsource the responsibility for exercising peripheral vision to external consultants, who can offer insights on the factors that could transform the firm's business. While these outside partners can provide fresh perspectives on the business, the company must pay careful attention to coordination to ensure that these "private eyes" are focused on the right areas and that the information is shared throughout the organization.

## Create a Coherent View

In this book, we have looked at seven steps that can improve the process of organizational peripheral vision and build capabilities and leadership that contribute to it. As we have repeatedly noted, however, peripheral vision entails a set of highly iterative processes. Scanning affects scoping, which in turn affects interpreting, probing, and acting. While we have separated these stages of peripheral vision for the purpose of exposition, this is not how challenges are presented to managers in practice. The stages are interrelated—vision and action occur in real time, and the time available for assessment and reaction is limited. In human vision, it is one thing to understand the process of vision and quite another to bring it all together to complete a successful jump shot on a basketball court. The same is true in organizations.

The iterative nature of peripheral vision can be envisioned as a set of interrelated questions, as shown in figure 8-1. We start by asking, What are the right questions to focus on? By exercising this curiosity, the organization begins to identify possible answers, decides what it has learned, and acts on this knowledge. Smart organizations will also reflect on where they are weak, based on past blind spots or missed opportunities. As they look to the periphery, managers must ask these questions:

- What questions should we ask (defining the scope)?

- How should we find the answers (determining scanning strategies)?

- What does it mean (making sense of the initial results)?

- What should we do (developing flexible postures for action)?

At the center is a process of defining how and where to scan the periphery. By asking and answering each of these questions, the

**FIGURE 8-1**

**Probing and learning about the periphery**

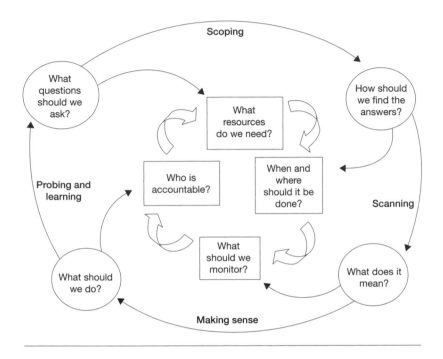

organization gains insight into the periphery and raises new questions that can deepen its peripheral vision.

This questioning process is supported by a set of organizational questions, as shown at the center of the figure, about what to monitor, where and when it should be done, who is responsible, and what resources are needed. The answers to these questions will shape how managers look at the periphery.

Finally, organizations must balance peripheral vision with focal vision to develop a coherent image of the world. It is the organization and, particularly, its top leaders that bring together and balance these two ways of looking at the world. Leaders decide how resources should be devoted for best effect and how insights from the periphery and focal business can be integrated.

# Survival of the Most Responsive

Somewhere in your organization there is probably someone who knows about a weak but potentially important signal of changes on the periphery. But how well is your organization designed to capture and share this insight? All of us have limits—individually and in our organizations—in how far we can see and in our ability to detect and act on weak signals at the periphery. Inevitably, some signals will be missed because recognizing them would require an ability to see through walls. Superheroes with x-ray vision currently exist only in science fiction and comic books.

We also must recognize that peripheral vision is different than focal vision. The process of peripheral vision requires different capabilities and approaches than focal vision. The signals are less clear, and this requires a different type of attention. Peripheral vision does not happen automatically in organizations; it requires resources and attention to improve their peripheral vision.

While the complexity of peripheral vision may defy simple recipes, our work makes it clear that peripheral vision can be strengthened using the strategies and frameworks presented in this book. Even though you cannot see through walls, you can recognize what is coming more quickly than your rivals.

Like being aware that a sudden outflow of the tide is a sign of a coming tsunami, recognizing these warning signs early can mean life or death. Organizations effective in building peripheral vision can gain tremendous advantages over their rivals. They can recognize and act on opportunities more quickly. They can avoid being blindsided by the market, technology, regulations, and competitors. It takes skill to do this well, but as the environment moves more quickly and becomes more uncertain, the payoffs from strong peripheral vision will be greater than ever. As Charles Darwin observed, "It's not the strongest of the species who survive, nor the most intelligent, but the ones most responsive to change."

# Strategic Eye Exam

## What's Your Organization's Vigilance Gap?

T HE FOLLOWING Strategic Eye Exam (assessment tool A-1) is designed to help management teams better understand what is meant by peripheral vision. Also, the survey measures the gap between an organization's need for peripheral vision and its ability to sense weak signals from its environment. Your need will depend on your strategy, the nature of your business, and your industry environment. Your capacity for peripheral vision is determined by your strengths in the five factors identified in chapter 7. While the exam can be completed by a single individual, it may be more revealing to get the views from several top managers or an even broader group. We suggest the following approach.

1. Ask the members of the senior management team to answer questions on the Strategic Eye Exam individually.

2. Each item of the exam is scored from 1 to 7. Complete all items for Part I (Need) and then Part II (Capability) for each executive.

3. Look for significant differences in scores among the members of the team and discuss why these discrepancies might have occurred.

4. By looking at both the overall scores for Need (section D) and Capacity (section J) and at the individual questions, try to arrive at a consensus judgment (or, if this seems impossible, just average the scores across team members).

5. Add up the scores for sections A, B, and C to get a total score for Need, and add up sections E through I to get a total score for Capability.

6. Use figure A-1 to determine whether your organization is vulnerable, vigilant, focused, or neurotic. Your two totals will place your organization into one of these four quadrants. A score of 96 on Need separates high from low. A score of 80 is the cutoff value for the Capability dimension.

7. If your organization is vigilant or focused, it need not do anything at present, although the organization should stay alert for changes in the environment that may increase its need for peripheral vision. If your organization is neurotic, it should look for ways to increase its focus. If your organization is vulnerable, it should actively cultivate better peripheral vision, beginning with the questions outlined in this exam and the strategies discussed in this book.

**FIGURE A-1**

## Peripheral vision and the environment

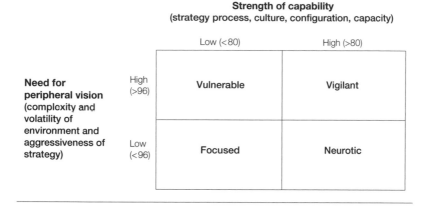

8. You can receive benchmarking data about how your scores compare to over 150 other companies by taking the survey electronically at www.thinkdsi.com.

## Strategic Eye Exam

Whether your organization's peripheral vision needs to change depends upon your current capability as well as the need for peripheral scanning given your strategy, the nature of your business, and your industry environment.

Using the scores of the following Strategic Eye Exam, we can assess your organization's need to improve its peripheral vision. Please answer as honestly and completely as you can.

ASSESSMENT TOOL A-1

## Strategic Eye Exam

*Before starting this survey, select the organizational perspective you are adopting:*

*A) Strategic Business Unit*
*B) Division*
*C) Entire Organization*
*D) Other*

### PART I: YOUR NEED FOR PERIPHERAL VISION

#### A. NATURE OF STRATEGY

| 1. Focus of your strategy | Narrow (protected niche) | 1 2 3 4 5 6 7 | Broad (global) |
|---|---|---|---|
| 2. Growth orientation | Modest and organic | 1 2 3 4 5 6 7 | Aggressive and acquisitive |
| 3. Number of businesses to integrate | Few | 1 2 3 4 5 6 7 | Many |
| 4. Focus on reinvention | Minor | 1 2 3 4 5 6 7 | Major (50 percent of revenue must come from new products in three years) |

#### B. COMPLEXITY OF YOUR ENVIRONMENT

| 1. Industry structure | Few, easily identifiable competitors | 1 2 3 4 5 6 7 | Many competitors from unexpected sources |
|---|---|---|---|
| 2. Channel structure | Simple and direct | 1 2 3 4 5 6 7 | Long and complex channel mix |
| 3. Market structure | Fixed boundaries and simple segmentation | 1 2 3 4 5 6 7 | Fuzzy boundaries and complex segmentation |
| 4. Enabling technologies | Few and mature (simple systems) | 1 2 3 4 5 6 7 | Many converging (complex systems) |
| 5. Regulations (federal, state, etc.) | Minimal or stable | 1 2 3 4 5 6 7 | Many or changing rapidly |
| 6. Public visibility of industry (media) | Largely ignored | 1 2 3 4 5 6 7 | Closely watched by media or special-interest groups |
| 7. Dependence on government funding and political access | Low: operates largely independent of government | 1 2 3 4 5 6 7 | High: sensitive to politics and funding climate |
| 8. Dependence on global economy | Low: domestic focus and isolated | 1 2 3 4 5 6 7 | High: affected by global conditions |

## Strategic Eye Exam *(continued)*

C. VOLATILITY OF YOUR ENVIRONMENT

| | | | |
|---|---|---|---|
| 1. Number of surprises by high-impact events in past three years | None | 1 2 3 4 5 6 7 | Three or more |
| 2. Accuracy of past forecasts | High: small deviations from actual | 1 2 3 4 5 6 7 | Low: actuals differ greatly from forecasts |
| 3. Market growth pattern | Slow and stable | 1 2 3 4 5 6 7 | Rapid and unstable |
| 4. Growth opportunities | Have decreased dramatically in the past three years | 1 2 3 4 5 6 7 | Have increased dramatically in past three years |
| 5. Speed and direction of technological change | Predictable | 1 2 3 4 5 6 7 | Unpredictable |
| 6. Behavior of key competitors, suppliers, and partners | Very predictable | 1 2 3 4 5 6 7 | Highly unpredictable |
| 7. Posture of key rivals | Live-and-let-live mentality | 1 2 3 4 5 6 7 | Hostile (aggressive) |
| 8. Susceptibility to macroeconomic forces | Low sensitivity to price changes, currencies, business cycles, tariffs, etc. | 1 2 3 4 5 6 7 | High sensitivity to prices, currencies, business cycles, tariffs, etc. |
| 9. Dependence on financial markets | Low | 1 2 3 4 5 6 7 | High |
| 10. Customer and channel power | Low | 1 2 3 4 5 6 7 | High |
| 11. Sensitivity to social changes (fashion, values) | Low: mostly gradual change from the past | 1 2 3 4 5 6 7 | High: good chance of major disruptions and changes in business models |
| 12. Potential for major disruptions over next five years | Low: few surprises expected; mostly things we can handle | 1 2 3 4 5 6 7 | High: several significant business shocks are expected, without our knowing which in particular |

D. SELF-ASSESSED OVERALL NEED FOR PERIPHERAL VISION

| | | | |
|---|---|---|---|
| 1. Today (at present) | Low | 1 2 3 4 5 6 7 | High |
| 2. During the past five years | Low | 1 2 3 4 5 6 7 | High |
| 3. Over the next five years | Low | 1 2 3 4 5 6 7 | High |

*(continued)*

---

## Strategic Eye Exam *(continued)*

### PART II: YOUR CAPACITY FOR PERIPHERAL VISION

#### E. LEADERSHIP ORIENTATION

| | | | |
|---|---|---|---|
| 1. Importance of periphery in business leader's agenda | Low priority | 1 2 3 4 5 6 7 | High priority |
| 2. Time horizon overall | Emphasis on short term (two years or less) | 1 2 3 4 5 6 7 | Emphasis on long term (5 or more years) |
| 3. Attitude toward the periphery in the organization | Limited and myopic (few people care) | 1 2 3 4 5 6 7 | Active and curious (systematic mining of periphery) |
| 4. Willingness to test and challenge basic assumptions | Mostly defensive | 1 2 3 4 5 6 7 | Very willing to test key premises or widely held views |

#### F. STRATEGY MAKING

| | | | |
|---|---|---|---|
| 1. Experience with uncertainty-reducing strategies (i.e., real options) | Limited | 1 2 3 4 5 6 7 | Extensive |
| 2. Use of scenario thinking to guide strategy process | Never | 1 2 3 4 5 6 7 | Frequent |
| 3. Number of alliance partners | Few | 1 2 3 4 5 6 7 | Many |
| 4. Flexibility of strategy process | Rigid, calendar driven, budgeting | 1 2 3 4 5 6 7 | Flexible, issues-oriented processes |
| 5. Resources devoted to scanning the periphery | Negligible | 1 2 3 4 5 6 7 | Extensive |
| 6. Integration of customer and competitor information into future technology platforms and new product development plans | Poorly and sporadically integrated | 1 2 3 4 5 6 7 | Systematically and fully integrated |

## Strategic Eye Exam *(continued)*

### G. KNOWLEDGE MANAGEMENT SYSTEM
#### (ESPECIALLY COMPETITIVE INTELLIGENCE/CUSTOMER DATABASES)

| | | | |
|---|---|---|---|
| 1. Quality of data about events and trends at the periphery | Poor: limited coverage and often out-of-date | 1 2 3 4 5 6 7 | Excellent: broad coverage and timely |
| 2. Access to data across organizational boundaries | Difficult: limited awareness of what is available | 1 2 3 4 5 6 7 | Relatively easy: wide awareness of what is available |
| 3. Use of database for existing business | Limited | 1 2 3 4 5 6 7 | Extensive |
| 4. Technologies for posing queries to databases | Old and difficult to use | 1 2 3 4 5 6 7 | State-of-the-art inquiring systems |

### H. CONFIGURATION (STRUCTURE AND INCENTIVES)

| | | | |
|---|---|---|---|
| 1. Accountability for sensing and action on weak signals | No one is responsible | 1 2 3 4 5 6 7 | Responsibility is clearly assigned to project team or dedicated group |
| 2. Early warning systems and procedures | None | 1 2 3 4 5 6 7 | Extensive and effective |
| 3. Incentives to encourage and reward wider vision | None | 1 2 3 4 5 6 7 | Top management recognition and direct rewards |

### I. CULTURE (VALUES, BELIEFS, AND BEHAVIORS)

| | | | |
|---|---|---|---|
| 1. Readiness to listen to reports from scouts on the periphery | Closed: listening discouraged | 1 2 3 4 5 6 7 | Open: listening encouraged |
| 2. Willingness of customer-contact people to forward market information | Poor | 1 2 3 4 5 6 7 | Excellent |
| 3. Sharing of information about periphery across functions | Poor: information ignored or hoarded | 1 2 3 4 5 6 7 | Excellent: ongoing information sharing at multiple levels |

### J. OVERALL PERIPHERAL VISION CAPABILITY

| | | | |
|---|---|---|---|
| 1. At present— today | Low | 1 2 3 4 5 6 7 | High |
| 2. Five years ago | Low | 1 2 3 4 5 6 7 | High |

## Comparative Results of the Strategic Eye Exam

We drew from many sources in designing the Strategic Eye Exam, including our own work on assessing organizational capabilities, especially the capabilities to sense the market and manage uncertainty (some of which are described in appendix B). The scales we developed are designed to overcome a persistent problem of survey measurements, namely that different respondents may use a different context when answering a question. By giving concrete descriptions of the end points of each scale, we help the respondents understand what we mean and thus anchor their answers in a common framework.

We designed this assessment tool so it would meet the customary requirements of construct validity, internal consistency, and external validity.[1] To better understand the survey's underlying structure, we tested the Strategic Eye Exam with more than 150 managers from diverse companies that were participating in executive programs at Wharton and Cedep at Insead, as well as 50 senior managers from a highly respected global manufacturing firm (to assess within-company results).

The Strategic Eye Exam presents a granular view of our two focal concepts, Need and Capability, and lists multiple items even if there is some overlap and correlation with other items. By retaining multiple items, we acknowledge that both capabilities and environment entail multiple facets that are embedded and interwoven. A standard Varimax rotation factor analysis confirmed that there was no strong overlap in these dimensions. It revealed no clear underlying structure in which a few basic factors explain either the environment or capability items well. Both are complex, multivariate constructs. Thus, we felt it better to keep a number of items to capture the many facets and complexities of the periphery. We also added sections D (for Need) and J (for Capacity) to derive holistic measures and compare them across time.

The most interesting findings came from the regression of the individual Need and Capability items on the respective overall judgments by the managers who completed this survey. The primary correlates of the overall Need for peripheral vision over the next five years (D3) were, in order of statistical significance:

- C2: The potential for major disruptions over the next five years (the mean was 4.2 out of 7, but the standard deviation was 1.5) $(p < .007)$

- A4: Focus on reinvention $(p < .02)$

- C6: Behavior of key competitors $(p < .06)$

- B7: Dependence on government funding $(p < .08)$

The most important correlates of the present peripheral vision Capability (J1) were:

- E3: (Leadership) attitude toward the periphery $(p < .004)$

- I3: Sharing of information $(p < .05)$

- H3: Incentives to encourage and reward wider vision $(p < .05)$

Our treatment in the book reflects these correlates, particularly the discussion of the components of a capability for peripheral vision (chapter 7).

# Research Foundation

THIS APPENDIX summarizes the scholarly underpinnings and background of our approach.[1] Because no generally accepted model of peripheral vision in organizations exists, to our knowledge, we synthesized ideas and insights from multiple disciplines.[2] Among our many sources, we drew insights from the fields of decision making, marketing, strategy, organization theory, and economics, as well as from more applied areas such as scenario planning, competitive intelligence, market research, environmental scanning, and technology forecasting.

Our conceptual model of peripheral vision is grounded in a particular view of organizational learning, as shown in figure B-1. This model reflects the descriptive realities of organizational learning but serves a prescriptive purpose in our book.[3] Our approach to organizational learning integrates highly normative models about developing new knowledge and collective insights with descriptive models of how individuals and organizations actually process information.[4]

**FIGURE B-1**

**Peripheral vision as a learning process**

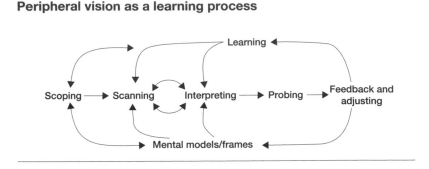

Our overall approach is straightforward. We assume that individuals are the receptors of the organization and that the organization's internal processes ultimately dictate what issues receive attention. Serious challenges reside at the individual, group, and organizational levels in surfacing the right issues at the right time. To appreciate these issues, we have incorporated various known biases of judgment and choice at the individual level with organizational and strategic dynamics at the firm level. Two broad intellectual paradigms underlie our approach to peripheral vision. The first is an information-processing paradigm of both individual and organizational decision making. The second is a complementary learning paradigm that examines how well or poorly complex enterprises adapt to an ever-changing environment. Let's briefly review each paradigm and then relate them to our particular model for improving peripheral vision.

## Information-Processing Paradigm

Ever since the classic work of Alan Newell and Herbert Simon on human problem solving, many scholars of administrative behavior have been partial to an information-processing view of organizational decision making.[5] This paradigm was applied organizationally in the classic work by Richard Cyert and James March and later by March and Johan Olsen, as well as many others.[6] James Thompson, John Steinbruner, and Jay Galbraith adopted a cybernetic view of organizations in trying to explain the wide variety of organizational design forms observed across markets and over time.[7] George Huber similarly used this model to understand organizational decision making and strategy.[8] Thanks to Newell and Simon, the information-processing paradigm also achieved great prominence at the individual level where cognitive psychologists envisioned the brain as a computer with limited storage, retrieval, and computing power.[9] Daniel Kahneman and Amos Tversky built on this approach when studying the nature of search and estimation procedures employed in judgment and choice.[10] The heuristic nature of human reasoning stands as a dominant theme in cognitive psychology, although deep, unresolved issues remain about the interplay of emotion and cognition at both the deliberative and subconscious levels.

When applied to the problem of peripheral vision, the information-processing paradigm suggests four key stages: perception, judgment, action, and feedback. At the organizational level, the parallel stages of this process can be described as information acquisition, information dissemination, shared interpretation, coordinated action, and collective learning. We can generate many variations around this basic framework, differing by type of learning (Is it adaptive or generative?), number of stages (Is dissemination part of interpretation?), and the role of mental representation (pattern recognition versus purposive construction). Enduring research questions remain about the mix of deliberative versus unconscious cognitive processing at each stage; the influence of heuristics and biases; and the role of schemata, mental models, and other simplifying frameworks for interpretation.

In recognition of the difference between learning from the periphery and learning within the focal area of the organization, we have extended the basic process to incorporate scoping—deciding where to look—as an explicit, rather than implicit, forerunner to the information acquisition or scanning stage. The scan within the initial scope can be passive or active depending on whether the organization waits for information to come to it or launches a directed inquiry. The next step is disseminating and interpreting the information to draw out useful insights. Last, an assessment must be made about whether the information should be used now, stored, or ignored, followed by learning from whatever action was taken. At all stages, the process is guided by a set of mental models or frames that reside deep within the organization.

## Organizational Learning Paradigm

The second major intellectual perspective that shaped our approach to peripheral vision is the organizational learning paradigm, which has many antecedents as well as points of intersection with the information-processing view. Peter Senge's book *The Fifth Discipline* might be viewed as a turning point in bringing an appreciation of the importance of a learning focus to a broad management audience.[11] Senge builds on prior work by Kurt Lewin, Edgar Schein, James March, and others, combining these insights with other viewpoints, notably the importance of systems thinking, into a full-fledged view of the learning organization. Related work by John Sterman, Chris Argyris, and others further helped shape organizational learning as a distinct intellectual perspective. The basic view is that learning is complex, not simple or automatic, in dynamic environments.[12] Ambiguous feedback, delayed reactions, multiple partial causation, self-serving attributions, missing data, treatment effects, random noise, and illusions of control all plague organizational attempts to figure out what happened and why.

When we add the low probability and ambiguous nature of peripheral signals, the problem is greatly compounded. Hillel Einhorn and Robin Hogarth, among others, have demonstrated that people exhibit strong ambiguity aversion when facing choices involving unknown risks.[13] People prefer the devil they know over the one they don't. Consequently, they neither dwell nor learn well in environments of high ambiguity. This bias may be exacerbated at the organizational level, where rationality and predictability are expected and desired. Yet new opportunities often entail a high level of uncertainty and consequently demand a high tolerance for ambiguity. To design cultures that can learn in complex environments may require different management principles and values than those needed to maximize the mainstream organization. Thus, a conflict arises between the learning and performance cultures within organizations, and senior management must find the right balance.

To acknowledge the crucial role of learning in improving peripheral vision, our model contains multiple feedback loops. We tried to capture the complex steps humans and organizations go through, from initial stimulus to final response, which involves much iterative learning. In the book, we have suffused each phase and feedback loop with insights and remedies from such fields as decision sciences, organization theory, strategy, marketing, and sociology. While there have been extensive studies of individual and organizational learning, the advice developed in the core areas of these disciplines may not readily extend to the periphery where, by definition, conscious attention and inference are limited. Consequently, we view the advice from the aforementioned fields as normative beacons that may provide only limited guidance.

## Stages of the Learning Process

While research on information processing and organizational learning informed our work more broadly, we also drew on diverse fields in understanding and addressing each stage of the learning process (see figure B-1).

## Scoping

How broadly should the field of view be defined? By definition, peripheral vision requires a broad definition of scope, stretching beyond the focal area of the organization. Hence, it entails paying attention to many areas that the organization might typically ignore. With a recognition of the cost of this broader focus, the challenge is to expand the scope just enough to include all the relevant parts of the environment but no more than this (see figure B-2). In general, the more uncertain the environment, the more likely there are to be threats from the periphery and the broader the scope that is needed.

There is an important parallel between the scoping and scanning decision and the extensive work on search rules in economics and operations research. When George Stigler wrote his seminal articles on the economics of information in the early 1960s, he examined the case of a consumer trying to find the best price for some common item.[14] He assumed that prices for this commodity varied across stores according to a known probability distribution and then

**FIGURE B-2**

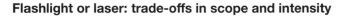

## Flashlight or laser: trade-offs in scope and intensity

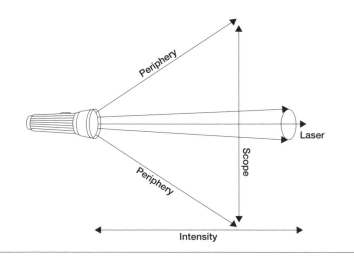

asked how many stores a consumer should visit, at random, to find the best price. Stigler then calculated, before starting the trip, the optimal number of stores to visit. The optimal point is where the marginal cost of visiting one more store exceeds the expected benefit in price reduction. Others have expanded on Stigler's work by recognizing that it would be suboptimal for a consumer to precommit to a fixed number of stores prior to embarking on the random search process.[15] Because the fixed optimum is predicated on a presumed prior distribution of price differences, the very act of sampling allows for an updating of that prior distribution. Thus, the optimal strategy is to solve the search problem anew after learning the price offered at a new store, in line with a Bayesian updating process. This flexible search rule is, of course, much more complex, but it also produces better results.

Scoping and scanning tasks are similarly related. There is an initial scoping decision based on the best available information about the distribution of relevant signals in the external environment. Then the firm scans within that scope and learns more about the actual signal-to-noise ratio based on its sampling. This should, in turn, lead to a revision of the scope in as far as the sampling data is significantly at odds with the presumed a priori density function. For an optimal search, we need variable rules rather than fixed rules.

We can even argue that the firm should sample beyond its optimal scope, just to validate its scoping boundary. It should find a low signal-to-noise ratio beyond the boundary and, if it cannot, it should reset the boundary. All scoping decisions should be tentative, subject to revision as new information is acquired. The low signal-to-noise ratio makes this continuous updating hard to model. The problem is akin to insurance companies that specialize in truly low-probability events (such as the one-hundred-year flood, an extreme earthquake, or a meltdown of a nuclear power plant) trying to update their underwriting models based on the very rare occurrence of a catastrophic loss. Ultimately, we must rely here on the judgments of the senior managers.

In establishing the scope of its learning, the organization needs to conduct an initial assessment of the environment to determine where relevant threats and opportunities may come from. A scenario-based strategic planning process can be a valuable tool in scoping as well as in making sense of and acting on weak signals from the periphery.[16] This helps determine the broadest possible relevant scope in terms of time frame, market view, technology perspective, economic and political issues, legal and environmental concerns, and other factors.

## Scanning

Once the scope is set, learning begins with scanning. This scanning can be focused on exploitation or exploration.[17] A mind-set of exploitation leads to directed searches within a well-defined and reasonably familiar domain. Exploratory scanning, in contrast, emphasizes the periphery further out and is driven by the kind of intense curiosity typical of true learning organizations.[18] The challenge here is to have an open mind and a broad view.

Exploratory scans can either be active or passive. In the passive mode, the management team keeps its antennae up and waits to receive outside signals. Although the organization may seem in tune with the periphery under this approach, it may not really be. Because most data comes from familiar or traditional sources, this mode of scanning tends to reinforce rather than challenge prevailing beliefs. The danger of this passive stance is that it filters out unexpected weak signals or even fails to receive them.

Active scanners have specific questions that they want to answer about the periphery they are exploring. Such scanning is hypothesis driven, and if complex issues are involved, multiple hypotheses should be tested.[19] Organizations engaged in active scanning are more likely to mount search parties using teams of outsiders and insiders, deploying a wide range of methods.

Exploratory scanning covers more ground but with less detail, making it efficient for broad-brush, big-picture views of the world. Exploitation scanning, in contrast, requires greater depth and related resources to mine deeply. What is the right balance between scanning for exploration and exploitation? One possible approach is to pay attention to *both* the detail and the big picture, using a strong top-down vision to identify areas that need more attention. This strategy requires resources for learning at greater distances from the focal vision, while also having a mechanism for triggering more focused attention if needed. (The FBI's use of "splatter vision," discussed in chapter 3, is an example of this approach.)

Our discussion of scanning approaches for different parts of the periphery (chapter 3) draws on diverse sources:

- *Customers and channels.* George Day's *The Market-Driven Organization* offers an overview of approaches to sensing changes in customers and channels, with references to other works.[20] For example, firms that are actively seeking new product opportunities at the periphery of their market scope may employ lead-user analysis, metaphor elicitation, and other techniques for surfacing latent needs. Gerald Zaltman offers a variety of approaches for identifying latent needs.[21] A growing body of research has found that market-driven firms usually are more profitable than their rivals, a conclusion that has been sustained with a variety of measures and methods.[22] One illustrative study found that market-driven businesses were 31 percent more profitable than self-centered firms, while those that were customer-oriented but didn't pay attention to competitors were 18 percent more profitable than those that were self-centered.[23]

- *Competitors and complementors.* There is an extensive literature on competitive intelligence that is largely (and appropriately) about understanding the capabilities and intentions of the focal competitors.[24] We have built on this work in looking at competitors at the periphery.

- *Technologies.* There are a variety of strategies for scanning and developing emerging technologies. Our discussion draws on insights from academic experts and practitioners in diverse areas in *Wharton on Managing Emerging Technologies*, based on the work of Wharton's William and Phyllis Mack Center for Technological Innovation.[25]

## Interpreting

Organizations should, in principle, be more effective than individuals at developing multiple hypotheses about the meaning of weak signals. Unfortunately, however, organizational sense making is usually driven toward one single meaning. How we interpret signals is deeply affected by our mental models or frames of mind and these, in turn, influence our hypotheses and inquiries going forward. So, the cognitive challenges at the periphery are far greater than in our focal areas because there is less data to work with and more room for bias and distortion to trip us up. For example, to appreciate the potential or threat from the periphery may require a shift in our mental models. We need to be prepared to make creative leaps and engage in prior brainstorming about possibilities. This requires a less rigid and formalized approach to filtering than we would apply to focal areas.

Ironically, one of the biggest impediments to the creative interpretation of the periphery is the urge to impose too much order on an inherently ambiguous picture. Because humans dislike ambiguity, we tend to quickly lock in on a view of the world. Once this lock takes place—as when one interpretation of an optical illusion snaps into focus—it is very difficult to reverse the process and not see the image we have interpreted. The ability to suspend focus or judgment and switch among different views is key to interpreting the periphery. Organizations often try to make too much sense of an inherently noisy environment. They would be better off developing multiple views.

## Probing and Acting

While organizations need to look and interpret broadly, they also need to be much more cautious about acting on input from the periphery. As discussed in chapters 5 and 6, there are three primary approaches to responding to weak signals from the periphery:[26]

- *Watch and wait.* This passive approach is appropriate when there is a high uncertainty due to conflicting information or the firm has the resources to be a fast follower and let others take the lead. As Constaninos Markides and Paul Geroski point out, being a "fast second" is sometimes more financially rewarding than being a first mover.[27] However, the challenge of this posture is not to overdo it so that it becomes an excuse to ignore external developments. This will make the organization a slow follower. The real challenge is to examine each weak signal in terms of its potential impacts and associated probabilities. This will require some conceptual debate among people familiar with the situation and possibly a full-blown decision tree analysis when things get complex (i.e., multiple uncertainties are involved as well as downstream decisions). The value of new information, which may be obtained through further action or simply the passage of time, can be assessed in a formal manner.[28]

- *Probe and learn.* As uncertainty lessens or the cost of inaction increases, a more aggressive approach is needed.[29] This can range from directed market explorations with advanced research methods to the negotiation of real option agreements to ensure the rights of first refusal to an emerging technology.[30] The goal of these initiatives is to create or acquire real options. While it takes some time and attention to evaluate options once they are generated, organizations generally do not suffer from the problem of generating too large and rich an array of options. Most often, they suffer from a paucity of creative options. It is not possible here to review the rich set of techniques for effective brainstorming, creativity, or options generation, but these approaches can significantly expand your pool of possible options.[31]

- *Believe and lead.* Full-scale commitment is warranted when the opportunity is very promising or the threat is imminent, and the organization is sufficiently persuaded by the available evidence. To justify this riskier posture requires a convergence of signals from the periphery and support for the assumptions that favor bold action. It also requires assessment of the risks of acting, or not acting, based on the often fuzzy input from the periphery.

For all three of these postures, the organization needs to develop capabilities for flexible response. Among the approaches that can help in acting fast and flexibly are creating a sense-and-respond management style; de-risking through fast prototyping, small experiments and networking; adopting an options perspective when acting on the periphery (developing a portfolio of options rather than placing one big bet); and practicing organizational agility.

## Learning and Adjusting

Once we act and start to obtain feedback, opportunities for learning and adjustment will arise. Infants refine their vision and actions by reaching out and touching the things they see. The interaction among organizational actions, perceptions, and reactions will refine the organization's understanding of its environment. Depending on the type of feedback it receives, an organization's deeper image of the world may need to be adjusted and the organization may need to shift its focal vision.

Because organizational processes for sense making and decision making are highly affected by managers' mental models, learning at the periphery may require a deeper change in these mental models as well. Rather than solving well-defined problems in a linear way using the convergent power of analysis, peripheral learning requires lateral thinking, asking disconfirming questions, relying on intuition, and looking at data through multiple lenses. This requires an ongoing, iterative process of scoping, scanning, interpreting, acting, learning, and adjusting by which individuals and organization define and shift their vision. This process has many feedback loops and is decidedly nonlinear. The results are a better understanding of the current periphery and a process for shifting the periphery toward the center of vision if needed.

## Vigilant Organizations

Capabilities are a bundle of closely integrated skills, technologies, and cumulative learning that are so deeply embedded in the organization that they cannot be traded or imitated.[32] The discussion of vigilant organizations draws on our Strategic Eye Exam and a variety of studies that have looked at important characteristics of companies operating in fast-paced environments or organizations that are designed for learning.[33] David DeLong and Liam Fahey discuss the importance of culture and its many facets, including values, norms, mental models, and behaviors.[34] There are trade-offs in different types of organizational cultures, and each has different mechanisms for processing and acting on information about the changing market environment.[35]

## Other Relevant Books

Finally, this work draws on many and diverse management books that have looked at the periphery from a number of perspectives (including competitive intelligence, market research, environmental scanning, and technology forecasting). The importance of watching the periphery has been emphasized in popular books such as Clayton Christensen's *The Innovator's Dilemma*, Andy Grove's *Only the Paranoid Survive*, and Richard Foster and Sarah Kaplan's *Creative Destruction*.[36] Malcolm Gladwell's best-selling *The Tipping Point* addressed the related phenomenon of peripheral products, ideas, or messages that sweep across society like epidemics thanks to informal networks of people.[37] Other books, such as Wayne Burkan's *Wide Angle Vision*, Ben Gilad's *Early Warning*, and Jim Harris's *Blindsided*, have also addressed aspects of this subject.[38]

There also are a number of academic works on related topics, such as Chun Wei Choo's *Information Management for the Intelligent Organization*; Karl Weick's classic *Sensemaking in Organizations*; and Weick's more recent work with Kathleen Sutcliffe, *Managing the Unexpected*.[39] An interesting collection of essays on weak signals and sense making is offered in Haridimos Tsoukas and Jill Shepherd's, *Managing the Future: Foresight in the Knowledge Economy*.[40] A historical account of governmental blind spots, and their various causes, is presented by Timothy Naftali's, *Blind Spot*.[41] This comprehensive book examines why national security officials missed warning signs in cases ranging from the Olympic Village massacre in Munich (1972) to the bombings of Marine headquarters in Beirut (1983) and the tragedy of 9/11 (2001). He also describes some foiled plots such as the attempted assassination of Eisenhower (1944) and the interception of terrorists targeting Los Angeles during the millennium celebration.

Clayton Christensen's more recent work with Scott Anthony and Erik Roth, *Seeing What's Next*, focuses on helping individual managers anticipate the evolution of disruptive technologies.[42] *Seeing What's Next* identifies specific patterns of industry disruption, whereas our book examines the processes and capabilities that organizations need to recognize such patterns or other significant changes in their environment. Max Bazerman and Michael Watkins's recent book, *Predictable Surprises*, explores the cognitive and social conditions that lead to missed signals, and W. Chan Kim and Renée Mauborgne's *Blue Ocean Strategy* highlights the opportunities in developing peripheral market spaces that are not recognized by industry incumbents.[43] Other books, such as Jerry Wind and Colin Crook's *The Power of Impossible Thinking*, emphasize the power of mental models in shaping the opportunities we see—or don't see—in work and life.[44]

These are just some of the many, diverse sources that have informed and inspired our discussions in the preceding chapters. This overview is not intended to be exhaustive—a near impossibility when it comes to a topic as broad and amorphous as the periphery. It is hoped, however, that our brief excursion through this background material will acknowledge the rich sources that have contributed to our understanding of this topic as well as point the way for readers who desire deeper explorations.

# Notes on Vision as a Metaphor for Organizations

ETAPHORS seek to highlight pertinent features of some phenomenon of interest through analogy and imagery. We all know that vision involves a complex process that extends far beyond the hardware features of the eye to the complex software that resides in the brain. By analogy, we view the organization as a complex entity in which sense making is conducted via input devices whose signals are then combined and synthesized into meaning. Because we use the metaphor of peripheral vision to explore this complex process in this book, let's briefly examine its salient features as well as its inherent limitations.

Most people, when hearing the term *peripheral vision*, associate it with perception from the corner of the eye. It is understood that this kind of vision is imprecise, as in a glance of the eye, and that unconscious processes largely dictate whether we give the peripheral signal further attention by turning our head. Because so many stimuli reach our peripheral retina, we can hardly afford to pay attention to each stimulus. Somewhere deep in the brain, it is decided what deserves attention, and this process is subject to limited strategic override. Nonetheless, when driving a car in busy city traffic, for example, we can prime ourselves to be on the lookout for bikers, children, or animals crossing the road, in addition to cars or motorcycles. Thus, we can create a strategic field of perception that affects both the aperture of our vision (how wide or narrowly we see) as well as the kind of peripheral signals that make it into our consciousness.

## How Vision Works

It is important to recognize that vision is different at the center of attention (the focal area) than at the periphery. As summarized in figure C-1, the nature of the signal, the accuracy of interpretation, and other characteristics of vision are quite different. There are different receptors in the eye for focal versus peripheral vision, with different profiles of strengths and weaknesses. Physiologically, the vision process begins with the activation of rod and cone cells, which are both sensitive to light but in different ways. While cone cells (used in focal vision) provide a clear image in living color, the rod cells (used in peripheral vision) are color-blind (which is why we don't detect color in dim lighting conditions). Humans have red, blue, and green cone cells, designed to absorb different wavelengths of light. The rod cells don't render precise images, but are good at detecting motion at the edge of our vision, functioning as perceptual outposts that are continually on the lookout for signals deserving further attention.

This hardware is only part of the story. Vision is the result of a complex process. When light bombards the eyes, the numerous rod and cone cells react without much filtering.[1] The initial image created from the visual field can be likened to the pixels on a computer

FIGURE C-1

## Differences in vision at the center and periphery

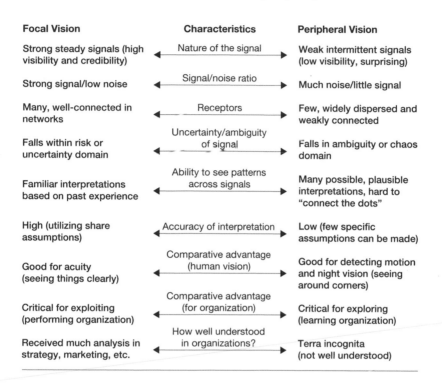

| Focal Vision | Characteristics | Peripheral Vision |
|---|---|---|
| Strong steady signals (high visibility and credibility) | Nature of the signal | Weak intermittent signals (low visibility, surprising) |
| Strong signal/low noise | Signal/noise ratio | Much noise/little signal |
| Many, well-connected in networks | Receptors | Few, widely dispersed and weakly connected |
| Falls within risk or uncertainty domain | Uncertainty/ambiguity of signal | Falls in ambiguity or chaos domain |
| Familiar interpretations based on past experience | Ability to see patterns across signals | Many possible, plausible interpretations, hard to "connect the dots" |
| High (utilizing share assumptions) | Accuracy of interpretation | Low (few specific assumptions can be made) |
| Good for acuity (seeing things clearly) | Comparative advantage (human vision) | Good for detecting motion and night vision (seeing around corners) |
| Critical for exploiting (performing organization) | Comparative advantage (for organization) | Critical for exploring (learning organization) |
| Received much analysis in strategy, marketing, etc. | How well understood in organizations? | Terra incognita (not well understood) |

screen that light up to varying degrees. This initial cycle of sensory perception is then followed by a second wave in which the mind seeks meaning, akin to an autofocus camera that is trying to find an object amid the many pixels. This second cycle is truly subjective in that it reflects the person's expectations, hopes, and fears. It relies heavily on pattern recognition, which functions as a type of mental software. If you are accustomed to seeing dogs rather than cats in your daily life, an ambiguous stimulus that could denote either would more likely be interpreted as a dog in the second cycle. There is frequent refreshing of the images created by the initial and secondary waves, with the frequency of updating (like a frame rate) dependent on how much change is occurring in the visual field. As these sequential frames are updated and refreshed, they compete for storage in visual memory, which is very much a winner-take-all process. The limits of visual memory are why we can only see part of the visual field clearly.

In human vision, this process works largely on automatic pilot. When you walk through a busy mall, most of the peripheral signals are filtered out, but an unusual, fast-moving image—such as a purse-snatcher running by—may draw sufficient attention to turn your head. Through evolution, the human eye has developed a suitable balance between peripheral and central signal processing, with far more cells devoted to the periphery than to focal vision. When predators lurk, all the eye needs is an early warning of approaching stripes and then the fight or flight response can set in after a more precise image has been obtained through the central (focal) vision.

Rods and cones are wired to other retinal neurons differently. For instance, up to one hundred rods may connect to a single ganglion cell.[2] As a result, the output of rods is considered as a whole, which leads to vision that is fuzzy and indistinct. In contrast, each cone in the fovea has a single, straight pathway to a ganglion cell. As a result, each cone essentially has its own "labeled line" to the higher visual centers. These "labeled lines" for the different senses help the brain differentiate sight, sound, smell, touch, and taste because the electrical impulses themselves are impossible to distinguish. A signal coming in from the optic nerve is thus interpreted as light. (This is why, if you receive a blow to the eye, it may initially be perceived as a flash of light rather than pain.)

In addition to vision, humans rely on four other senses that help round out the picture. Species differ, of course, in both the kind of sensory apparatus they possess and the importance accorded to each in case they offer conflicting information. Humans are strongly visually attuned compared, for instance, with bats or eels. Many nocturnal animals have only rod cells, which are better for seeing at night, but a hawk has more cone cells to sharply focus on prey on the ground below.

## Organizational Analogies

How should we construe the vision analogy in the context of an organization? One approach is to simplify the organization as a single entity (with a central brain) that sees certain parts of its environment very clearly, other parts dimly, and yet other parts not at all. The dimly perceived part constitutes the organization's periphery; much of it is ignored, but some is deemed worthy of attention. Unlike the human eye, where this attention-paying process is largely automatic and quick (i.e., we detect something in the corner of our eye and then take a closer look by turning our head or move on), the organization can be more deliberate about what and how it scans (a relative plus) but at the same time will be slower in turning its head due to organizational inertia (a relative minus). We could test these notions by measuring reaction time in an organization after new stimuli are introduced into its visual field. Whereas the human eye responds in a fraction of a second, organizational reaction times can range from hours (when in crisis mode) to weeks or even months when the signal is detected deep down in the organization or at the edge.

It is tempting to think of the people in the organization as being the rod and cone cells. But unlike rods and cones, which are physiologically limited and fixed in design, humans can to some extent perform both roles—enhancing focal vision and improving peripheral vision. Different jobs will require a different balance between cone- and rod-type functions, from a laser-beam focus on the task at hand to being a lookout post picking up signals from far afield and all around. An operations manager running a plant will typically need a narrower focus on performance, while a strategic planner engaged in creating scenarios or marketer hired as a cool hunter will necessarily have a strong peripheral focus. Humans have the capacity for both focal and peripheral vision, although to varying degrees, so they can change their attention from one to the other depending on their role.

Also, in organizations, the rods and cones exhibit much more interaction before passing the information on to the central processing unit of the brain. And it is not clear that we can usefully view an organization as experiencing pulsating waves that alternate between objective scans of the external stimuli and an interpretative wave that seeks meaning amid the animated pixel field. But, in some ways, organizations do try to scan their environment objectively, after which some interpretation and refreshing of the perceptual frame occurs. But the process is not as synchronized or unified as with human vision, where only one image is sought. So, we must avoid the fallacy of treating employees as rods or cones.

The most salient parts of the vision metaphor for our purposes are as follows:

1. Meaning is created from sensory inputs, which in turn prompt higher-level cognitive processes. The eyes are the input devices, and the brain the creator of meaning. In organizations, people function both as receptors and interpreters, resulting in a much more complex picture. The strategic challenge is to know where the weaknesses lie in organizations—do they see poorly, or do they interpret what everyone sees poorly?

2. The human eye has evolved such that neural receptor cells are specialized into two kind: cones for central vision and rods for the periphery. There are far more rods than cones, and they differ in the object features they respond to (in terms of color, shape, motion, etc.). This suggests that organizations may likewise need different receptors and design principles for central versus peripheral vision. It also raises the question of whether organizations should devote more resources to scanning the periphery.

3. The human eye can suffer from a variety of limitations and distortions (myopia, glaucoma, night blindness, etc.),

which result in distinct failures of perception. Often these distortions can be corrected. Organizations, likewise, may suffer from distinct vision problems that can often be corrected once they are understood.

4. Peripheral vision matters more in some tasks than in others. In fast-moving environments, such as sports or busy traffic on the road, peripheral vision matters more than good central vision. We can develop and train our peripheral vision (as Bill Bradley did in basketball) and then turn it into a competitive advantage. The key to good peripheral vision is to unfocus (splatter vision) prior to homing in and probing more deeply for better insight.

## Limits of the Metaphor

All metaphors have their limitations, and the differences highlight some distinctive features of organizational peripheral vision. Clearly, certain salient features of human vision—such as the distinction between central and peripheral vision—bear an analogy to organizational life. Companies and leaders see some things very clearly and others poorly. Likewise, peripheral vision is essential to both individuals and organizations—each needs some degree of peripheral vision to prosper. Where the metaphor breaks down is in the degree of strategic control that can be exerted. While humans can train their peripheral vision or artificially improve it by using side mirrors, glasses, or other sensing devices (such as night-vision goggles), the hardware for human vision is largely fixed (and, in fact, deteriorates). In contrast, organizations can very deliberately increase their visual aperture because they are less constrained by hardware limitations. Special teams, new data sources, strategy meetings, and focus groups can all be used to improve perception beyond the focal area of vision. This means that organizations have considerable flexibility in developing peripheral vision but they don't always exercise this flexibility. This may be because organizational evolution—unlike human evolution, which is designed for long-term survival of the species—typically is focused on short-term performance and survival. Investments in peripheral vision need to be balanced against investments that might produce more immediate returns.

The metaphor also breaks down when we examine the mapping of external stimuli onto meaning. In the eye, it is fairly clear whether a signal is peripheral or focal; it depends on the extent to which light waves activate rod or cone cells. The human eye has a mixture of rod and cone cells throughout, except in the central fovea, where cone cells are exclusively concentrated; that is, the ratio of cone to rod cells varies from very small to 100 percent as we move from the corner of the eye to the center. For an organization, we might, similarly, consider this to be a weighted average. For example, we could measure how many people registered a signal, to what extent that signal is central for each person concerned, and what power position or degree of centrality each person occupies in the organization. Then we could compute a weighted score in terms of how much a particular perception lies toward the peripheral versus central side of the scale. But this is rather forced, and the ratios can be changed by executive fiat (unlike the human eye). Our Strategic Eye Exam (see appendix A) measures how well developed various organizational capabilities are that support peripheral vision (relative to the need for it, which depends on the environment). Some of these capabilities operate at the level of cones and rods (i.e., better receptors in the organization), but most deal with the far more important level of interpretation and strategic probing. For this, leadership is needed above all. In organizations, as with human vision, the person at the center of this visual activity is largely responsible for what is seen, how it is interpreted, and what is done about it.

# Notes

*Introduction*

1. Leonard Fuld, "Be Prepared," *Harvard Business Review,* November 2003, 1–2. The survey was conducted by the Fuld-Gilad-Herring Academy of Competitive Intelligence.

2. See the acknowledgments for the names of the distinguished academics and practitioners who helped us on our journey of understanding.

*Chapter 1*

1. Andrew S. Grove, *Only the Paranoid Survive: How to Exploit the Crisis Points That Challenge Every Company* (New York: Currency Doubleday, 1999), 110.

2. All quotes from Mr. Melchiorre are based on personal communications with the authors.

3. Melanie Warner, "Low Carbs? Who Cares? Sugar Is the Latest Supermarket Demon," *New York Times*, May 15, 2005, 1.

4. Melanie Warner, "Is the Low-Carb Boom Over?" *New York Times*, December 5, 2004, Section 3, 1.

5. *The Vanishing Potato: Understanding the World of Low-Carb Dieting from a Consumer Perspective*, The Hartman Group, summer 2004.

6. A self-assessment survey using items scaled from 1 to 7. Statistics are based on responses from over 150 participants in senior management programs at Wharton and Cedep at Insead. The diagnostic Strategic Eye Exam used to estimate these results is in appendix A. The figure 80 percent is a comparison of the managers' future need for peripheral vision against their current capacity.

7. Sidney G. Winter, "Specialised Perception, Selection and Strategic Surprise: Learning from the Moths and Bees," *Long Range Planning* 37 (2004), 163–169.

8. Complex and fast-moving environments generally tend to push the limits of our vision. Astronauts reported that during rapid acceleration they felt as if they were slowly tilting backward. Changing magnetic fields produced a perception of luminous streaks and bright spots during the Apollo flights in the 1960s, and too much oxygen in the cabin produced tunnel vision, distorting the astronauts'

peripheral vision into a swirl of shapes. Because of such tricks caused by the environment, astronauts and jet pilots are taught not to trust their eyes alone but to use navigational systems to assess the craft's position. Discussed in Lael Wertenbaker, *The Eye: Window to the World* (New York: Torstar Books, 1984), 146.

9. See Manfred Kets de Vries and Danny Miller, *The Neurotic Organization: Diagnosing and Changing Counterproductive Styles of Management* (San Francisco: Jossey-Bass, 1984).

10. Focal vision is often referred to as "central vision" in ophthalmology. See, for example, Nicholas J. Wade and Michael Swanston, *Visual Perception* (East Sussex, UK: Psychology Press, 2001).

11. John McPhee, *A Sense of Where You Are: Bill Bradley at Princeton* (New York: Farrar, Straus and Giroux, 1999).

*Chapter 2*

1. Kathleen M. Sutcliffe and Klaus Weber, "The High Cost of Accurate Knowledge," *Harvard Business Review*, May 2003, 74–82.

2. Peter Schwartz, *The Art of the Long View: Planning for the Future in an Uncertain World* (New York: Currency Doubleday, 1996).

3. Some of these issues were suggested in a private discussion with Arthur Caplan, director of the Center for Bioethics at the University of Pennsylvania.

4. Stephen Baker and Adam Aston, "The Business of Nanotech," *Business-Week*, February 14, 2005, 71.

5. Stephan Herrera, "Mitsubishi: Out Front in Nanotech," *Technology Review*, January 2005, 34.

6. Max H. Bazerman and Michael D. Watkins, *Predictable Surprises: The Disasters You Should Have Seen Coming and How to Prevent Them* (Boston: Harvard Business School Press, 2004).

7. John Schwartz, "For NASA, Misjudgments Led to Latest Shuttle Woes," *New York Times*, July 31, 2005, Section 1, 1.

8. "How CEMEX Innovates," *Strategy & Innovation* (November–December 2004), 6–8.

9. Andrew S. Grove, *Only the Paranoid Survive: How to Exploit the Crisis Points That Challenge Every Company* (New York: Currency Doubleday, 1999).

10. Clayton M. Christensen, *The Innovator's Dilemma* (Boston: Harvard Business School Press, 1997); Clayton M. Christensen, Scott D. Anthony, and Erik A. Roth, *Seeing What's Next? Using the Theories of Innovation to Predict Industry Change* (Boston: Harvard Business School Press, 2004).

11. Michael E. Porter, *Competitive Advantage: Creating and Sustaining Superior Performance* (New York: Free Press, 1985).

12. Russell L. Ackoff, *Creating the Corporate Future: Plan or Be Planned For* (New York: John Wiley & Sons, 1981).

13. W. Chan Kim and Renée Mauborgne, *Blue Ocean Strategy: How to Create Uncontested Market Space and Make the Competition Irrelevant* (Boston: Harvard Business School Press, 2005).

14. Clayton M. Christensen and Michael E. Raynor, *The Innovator's Solution: Creating and Sustaining Successful Growth* (Boston: Harvard Business School Press, 2003).

15. Herman Kahn, *Thinking About the Unthinkable* (New York: Simon & Schuster, 1984).

16. Adrian Slywotzky, "Exploring the Strategic Risk Frontier," *Strategy & Leadership* 32 (2004), 11–19.

*Chapter 3*

1. G. K. Chesterton, *The Scandal of Father Brown* (New York: Dodd, Mead & Company, 1935).

2. This is also true of the fully developed system of metrics found in the Balanced Scorecard strategy map framework for illustrating how strategy links intangible assets to value-creating processes. See Robert S. Kaplan and David P. Norton, *Strategy Maps: Converting Intangible Assets into Tangible Outcomes* (Boston: Harvard Business School Press, 2004).

3. The case for having prior hypotheses was well made by James M. Utterback and James W. Brown, "Monitoring for Technological Opportunities," *Business Horizons,* October 1971, 5–15.

4. Wayne Burkan, *Wide-Angle Vision: Beat Your Competition by Focusing on Fringe Competitors, Lost Customers, and Rogue Employees* (New York: John Wiley & Sons, 1996), 85–86.

5. This section is adapted from "Market Sensing" in George S. Day, *The Market-Driven Organization* (New York: Free Press, 1999), chap. 5.

6. www.iconoculture.com.

7. For a deeper insight into these methods, see Gerald Zaltman, *How Customers Think: Essential Insights into the Mind of the Market* (Boston: Harvard Business School Press, 2003).

8. For a further introduction, see Stefan Thomke, "Note on the Lead User Research," teaching note 6-699-014, Harvard Business School; Eric von Hippel, Stefan Thomke, and Mary Sennack, "Creating Breakthroughs at 3M," *Harvard Business Review*, September–October 1999, 47–57.

9. Melanie Wells, "Have It Your Way" *Forbes*, February 14, 2005, 78–86.

10. Korea's broadband penetration has been accelerated by government support, a long history of cultural fascination with gaming, and world-class local electronics firms such as Samsung.

11. Malcolm Gladwell, "The Coolhunt," *The New Yorker*, March 17, 1997, 78–89.

12. Chidanand Apte, Bing Liu, Edwin P. D. Pednault, Padhraic Smyth, "Business Applications of Data Mining," *Communications of the ACM* 45 (August 2002): 49–53.

13. There is an extensive literature on competitive intelligence that is largely (and appropriately) about understanding the capabilities and intentions of the focal competitors. See Liam Fahey, *Competitors: Outwitting, Outmaneuvering, and Outperforming*

(New York: John Wiley, 1999); Leonard M. Fuld, *The New Competitor Intelligence: The Complete Resource for Finding, Analyzing, and Using Information About Your Competitors* (New York: John Wiley, 1994); John E. Prescott and Stephen H. Miller, eds., *Proven Strategies in Competitive Intelligence: Lessons from the Trenches* (New York: John Wiley, 2000).

14. W. Chan Kim and Renée Mauborgne, "Creating New Market Space," *Harvard Business Review*, January–February 1999, 83–93.

15. Gary Hamel and C. K. Prahalad, *Competing for the Future* (Boston: Harvard Business School Press, 1994).

16. The role of complementors gained wide visibility with Adam M. Brandenberger and Barry H. Nalebuff, *Co-Opetition* (New York: Doubleday, 1996).

17. In a 1968 video clip, Doug Engelbart demonstrates the use of a new computing device called the "mouse." It took several more decades for this computing device to change the personal computer interface, but it was there on film in 1968 if one had eyes to see it. See D. A. Levinthal, "The Slow Pace of Rapid Technological Change: Gradualism and Punctuation in Technological Change," *Industrial and Corporate Change* 7, no. 2 (1998): 217–247.

18. Don S. Doering and Roch Parayre, "Identification and Assessment of Emerging Technologies," in *Wharton on Managing Emerging Technologies*, ed. G. S. Day and Paul J. H. Schoemaker (New York: John Wiley & Sons, 2000), 75–98.

19. Ron Adler and Daniel A. Levinthal, " Technology Speciation and the Path of Emerging Technologies," in *Wharton on Managing Emerging Technologies*, 57–74.

20. Sherwin Nuland, "Do You Want to Live Forever?" *Technology Review* (February 2005): 36–45; see also Ray Kurzweil and Terry Grossman, *Fantastic Voyage: The Science Behind Radical Life Extension* (New York: Rodale Publishing, 2004).

21. Malcolm Gladwell, *The Tipping Point: How Little Things Can Make a Big Difference* (Boston: Little, Brown, 2000).

Chapter 4

1. The story about the tribal chief and the banana cart is recounted in Arie de Geus, *The Living Corporation* (Boston: Harvard Business School Press, 1997).

2. "A Vital Job Goes Begging," *New York Times*, February 12, 2005, A30.

3. Flo Conway and Jim Seligman, *Snapping: America's Epidemic of Sudden Personality Change* (Philadelphia: Lippincott, 1978).

4. Vincent Barabba, *Surviving Transformation: Lessons from GM's Surprising Turnaround* (New York: Oxford University Press, 2004).

5. These unmet needs were identified in a study by Wirthlin Worldwide through two measures: the importance consumers placed on key factors that influenced their buying decisions and their current level of satisfaction with these factors.

6. This is drawn from a study of how concepts and metaphors from the field of vision can be applied to competitive intelligence activities. See Michael Neugarten, "Seeing and Noticing: An Optical Perspective on Competitive Intelligence," *Journal of Competitive Intelligence and Management* 1, no. 1 (Spring 2003): 93–104.

7. Quoted in Michael Michalko, *Cracking Creativity* (Berkeley, CA: Ten Speed Press, 2001).

8. Adapted from George S. Day, "Assessing Future Markets for Emerging Technologies," in *Wharton on Managing Emerging Technologies*, ed. George S. Day and Paul J. H. Schoemaker (New York: John Wiley & Sons, 2000).

9. For a managerial overview of this extensive field, see J. Edward Russo and Paul J. H. Schoemaker, *Winning Decisions* (New York: Doubleday, 2001).

10. This brief discussion of groupthink draws on a more extensive summary offered in Russo and Schoemaker, *Winning Decisions*, chap. 7. The original and classic reference on groupthink is Irving Janis, *Groupthink: Psychological Studies of Policy Decisions and Fiascos*, 2nd ed. (Boston: Houghton Mifflin, 1982). For a critical review of groupthink as a psychological model, see Won-Woo Park, "A Review of Research on Groupthink," *Journal of Behavioral Decision Making* 3, no. 4 (October–December 1990): 229–246.

11. J. Patrick Wright, *On a Clear Day You Can See General Motors* (Grosse Pointe, MI: Wright Enterprises, 1979), 67–68.

12. Rational models from Bayesian analysis to bootstrapping can be used to form a judgment based on information from diverse sources. Bayesian analysis is a formal way of revising probability estimates after receiving new sampling information. This quantitative approach to decision making is further explained in Robert Nau and Robert Clemen, *Making Hard Decisions: An Introduction to Decision Analysis*, 2nd ed. (Boston: PWS-Kent, 1996); as well as the classic, Howard Raiffa, *Decision Analysis: Introductory Lectures on Choices Under Uncertainty* (Reading, MA: Addison-Wesley, 1968). Bootstrapping is the technique of building models of human experts and then outperforming them with that very same model on new predictions. The linear model that underlies most bootstrapping studies has a history of well over fifty years. A seminal work is Paul Meehl, *Clinical Versus Statistical Prediction* (Minneapolis: University of Minnesota Press, 1954). A primary contributor to the subsequent work is Robyn Dawes of Carnegie-Mellon University. Two of his papers are particularly accessible to nonprofessional readers: "Clinical versus Actuarial Judgment," written jointly with David Faust and Paul Meehl, *Science* 243 (1989): 1668–1673, and "The Robust Beauty of Improper Linear Models in Decision Making," *American Psychologist* 34 (1979): 571–582. An excellent review of bootstrapping studies is offered in Colin Camerer, "General Conditions for the Success of Bootstrapping Models," *Organizational Behavior and Human Performance* 27 (1981): 411–422. A thorough discussion of possible objections to using linear models is offered in Alison Hubbard Ashton, Robert H. Ashton, and Mary N. Davis, "White-Collar Robotics," *California Management Review* 37, no. 1 (Fall 1994): 95–101. The case for combining human judgment and statistical models has been well made by Robert Blattberg and Steven Hoch, "Database Models and Managerial Intuition: 50% Model + 50% Manager," *Management Science* 36, no. 8 (1990): 887–899.

13. Suppose you receive intriguing information about the actions of a new competitor from a colleague working in your own department, in another division,

or at another company. How much credence will you attach to this information in each case? One theory predicts that we undervalue information that originates from farther away (other things being equal) because of a "not invented here" syndrome, trust considerations, and clanlike behavior. However, another plausible view makes the opposite prediction, namely that we become complacent about those close to us (i.e., familiarity breeds contempt). Tanya Menon and other researchers have explored the impact of various relationships between the sender and receiver, including whether the sender is part of the work group or is a threat to the receiver in terms of career advancement. In one study, they find that external knowledge is valued more highly than internal knowledge because outsiders tend to enjoy higher status, offer information that is more scarce or novel, and be less of competitive threat within the organization. See Tanya Menon and Jeffrey Pfeffer, "Valuing Internal vs. External Knowledge: Explaining the Preference for Outsiders," *Management Science* 49, no.4 (2003), 497–513; Tanya Menon and Sally Blount, "The Messenger Bias," *Research in Organizational Behavior* 25 (2003): 137–186. See also M. B. Brewer and R. J. Brown, "Intergroup Relations," in *The Handbook of Social Psychology*, vol. 2, ed. Daniel T. Gilbert, Susan T. Fiske, and Gardner Lindzcy (Boston: McGraw-Hill, 1998), 554–594; R. S. Burt, *Structural Holes* (Cambridge, MA: Harvard University Press, 1992); R. B. Cialdini, *Influence* (Needham Heights, MA: Allyn & Bacon, 2001).

14. Larry Bossidy and Ram Charan, "Confronting Reality," *Fortune*, October 18, 2004, 225–229.

15. An excellent philosophical treatment of different approaches to gathering and interpreting information is C. West Churchman's classic book, *The Design of Inquiring Systems* (New York: Basic Books, 1971).

16. James Surowiecki, *The Wisdom of Crowds* (New York: Doubleday, 2004).

17. Michael Mavaddat, personal communication with authors, 2005.

18. Royal/Dutch Shell used scenario planning as a learning process to help surface the implicit mental models in its organization. This form of institutional learning can be seen as a way for management teams to "change their shared models of their company, their markets and their competitors." Arie de Geus, "Planning as Learning," *Harvard Business Review*, March–April 1988, 70–74.

19. Several sources cover the art and science of scenario planning. For a managerial introduction, see Paul J. H. Schoemaker, "Scenario Planning: A Tool for Strategic Thinking," *Sloan Management Review* (Winter 1995): 25–40. For a conceptual and behavioral perspective, see Paul J. H. Schoemaker, "Multiple Scenario Developing: Its Conceptual and Behavioral Basis," *Strategic Management Journal* 14 (1993): 193–213. For scenario planning books with applications in practice, see Peter Schwartz, *Art of the Long View* (New York: Currency Doubleday, 1991); Cees van der Heijden, *Scenarios: The Art of Strategic Conversation* (New York: John Wiley, 1996); Gill Ringland, *Scenario Planning* (New York: John Wiley, 1998); Liam Fahey and Robert Randall, eds., *Learning from the Future* (New York: John Wiley, 1998); Paul J. H. Schoemaker, *Profiting from Uncertainty* (New York: Free Press, 2002).

*Chapter 5*

1. All quotes from John Carmon are taken from personal communications with the authors.

2. Patricia Leigh Brown, "Eco-Friendly Burial Sites Give a Chance to Be Green Forever," *New York Times*, August 13, 2005, A1–A8.

3. Don S. Doering and Roche Parayre, "Identification and Assessment of Emerging Technologies," in *Wharton on Managing Emerging Technologies*, ed. G. S. Day and Paul J. H. Schoemaker (New York: John Wiley & Sons, 2000), 75.

4. This account is based on Peter Maass, "The Breaking Point," *New York Times Magazine*, August 21, 2005, 30–35.

5. Matthew R. Simmons, *Twilight in the Desert: The Coming Saudi Oil Shock and the World Economy* (New York: John Wiley & Sons, 2005).

6. G. Felda et al., "In-Q-Tel," Case 8-804-146 (Boston: Harvard Business School, 2004).

7. Microsoft was already playing many bets as early as 1988. At that time, Apple was at its peak with its superior graphical user interface for the Macintosh, making Microsoft's DOS look like a distant second. However, Microsoft was operating on multiple fronts. On one, it was developing Windows; on another, it was pushing OS/2, which it co-developed with IBM. And, at the same time, Microsoft was introducing various application software packages, including Excel and Word, for both Windows and Apple's Macintosh. Last, Microsoft was in partnership with SCO, the largest provider of PC-based Unix systems; see Eric D. Beinhocker, "Robust Adaptive Strategies," *Sloan Management Review* (Spring 1999): 95–106.

8. Rita Gunther McGrath and Ian C. MacMillan, "Discovery-Driven Planning," *Harvard Business Review*, July–August 1995, 44–54.

9. This section is largely adapted from John P. Ranieri, "Real Options in Action at DuPont," paper presented at the conference Investing in Emerging Technologies, November 21, 2003, University of Pennsylvania.

10. This section draws on Paul J. H. Schoemaker, "Deliberate Mistakes: How Two Wrongs Can Make a Right" (unpublished manuscript).

11. For further details, see J. L. Showers and L. M. Chakrin, "Reducing Uncollectible Revenues from Residential Telephone Customers," *Interfaces* 11 (1981): 21–31.

12. Arie de Geus, *The Living Organization* (Boston: Harvard Business School Press, 1997).

*Chapter 6*

1. In David Talbot, "LEDs vs. the Lightbulb," *Technology Review*, May 2003, 30–36.

2. Lighting Transformations, www.lrc.rpi.edu/programs/lightingTransformation/LED/issuesOptions02.asp

3. Bruce Sterling, "10 Technologies That Deserve to Die," *Technology Review*, October 2003, 52–55.

4. Statistic comes by Govi Rao and other resources at Philips Lighting Company.

5. All quotes in this chapter by Govi Rao are from personal communications with the authors.

6. Peter Svensson, "LED Evolution Could Replace Light Bulbs," Associated Press, April 15, 2005.

7. Mark Kendall and Michael Scholand, *Energy Savings Potential of Solid State Lighting Applications* (Arlington, VA: Arthur D. Little, 2001), 8.

8. Interview with Dr. Richard Stevens, University of Connecticut, during the *Bridges in Light Conference*, organized by the Lighting Research Center at Rensselaer Polytechnic Institute, Troy, NY, November 2004.

9. There is an extensive literature on the first-mover advantage. For an overview, see Gerard J. Tellis and Peter N. Golder, *Will and Vision* (New York: McGraw-Hill, 2002). As they point out, much of the early research that revealed a profit and share advantage to pioneers was based on studies of surviving firms. See, for example, Robert D. Buzzell and Bradley T. Gale, *The PIMS Principle: Linking Strategy to Performance* (New York: Free Press, 1987); Glen Urban et al., "Market Share Rewards to Pioneering Brands: An Empirical Analysis and Strategic Implications," *Management Science* 32 (1986): 645–659.

10. Constantinos C. Markides and Paul A. Geroski, *Fast Second: How Smart Companies Bypass Radical Innovation to Enter and Dominate New Markets* (San Francisco: Jossey-Bass, 2004).

11. Geoffrey A. Moore, *Crossing the Chasm* (New York: HarperBusiness, 1991).

12. Markides and Geroski, *Fast Second*.

13. Marvin B. Lieberman, and David B. Montgomery, "First-Mover Advantages," *Strategic Management Journal* 9 (1988): 41–58.

*Chapter 7*

1. "Is Barbie Past Her Shelflife?" *BBC News*, April 21, 2004.

2. Mel Duvall and Kim S. Nash, "Mattel: How Barbie Lost Her Groove," *Baseline*, August 4, 2005, www.baselinemag.com/article2/0,1397,1842984,00.asp.

3. Nicola Seare, "Barbie's Mid-Life Crisis," *BBC News*, July 21, 2004.

4. On Interbrand's list of the most valuable 100 global brands, Barbie dropped from 84 in 2001 to 97 in 2003 and a year later fell off the list completely. According to Interbrand estimates, the brand's value dropped from $2.23 billion in 2000 to $1.87 billion in 2003, in current dollars. In other words, the Barbie brand lost more than $360 million in value in two years.

5. Robert Cooper, *Winning at New Products: Accelerating the Process from Idea to Launch* (New York: Persus Publishing, 2001).

6. Mattel Annual Report, 2003, Form 10-K, p. 19

7. We purposely focus on organizational capabilities in this chapter because these tend to be a greater source of differentiation and advantage than hard assets,

which are readily available on the open market. Capabilities are deeply embedded in the organization, making them difficult to imitate, even when competitors can see them. For example, while most rivals could see Wal-Mart's logistics capabilities, they proved very difficult to replicate. Because capabilities tend to be difficult to imitate, they can be scarce, durable, and the source of superior profits. They tend to be specialized to a firm, making them difficult to trade or transfer. They are often complementary to one another, thus creating a system that can deliver above-average returns on investments. But capabilities must be well attuned to the nature and competitive structure of the firm's markets and industry. Capabilities must reflect and embody structural, political, *and* process advantages. See, for example, J. Barney, "Firm Resources and Sustained Competitive Advantage," *Journal of Management* 17, no. 1 (1991): 99–120; Raffi Amit and Paul J. H. Schoemaker, "Strategic Assets and Organizational Rent," *Strategic Management Journal* 14, no. 1 (1993), 33–46; D. J. Teece, G. Pisano, and A. Shuen, "Dynamic Capabilities and Strategic Management," *Strategic Management Journal* 18, no. 7 (1997): 509–533.

9. Peter Grant, "Comcast's Big Bet on Content," *Wall Street Journal*, September 24, 2004, p. B1.

9. "Mattel's New Toy Story," *BusinessWeek*, November 18, 2002, 72–73.

10. Mattel Annual Report, p. 83.

11. Michael Useem, *Leading Up: How to Lead Your Boss So You Both Win* (New York: Crown Business, 2001).

12. Jim Collins, *Good to Great: Why Some Companies Make the Leap . . . and Others Don't* (New York: HarperBusiness, 2001).

13. Jeffrey H. Dyer, Prashant Kale, and Harbir Singh, "How to Make Strategic Alliances Work," *Sloan Management Review* (Summer 2001): 37–43.

14. Warren Bennis, "It's the Culture," *Fast Company*, August 2003, 35.

15. Kathleen Eisenhardt from Stanford University has studied, with colleagues, how firms operating in high-velocity environments behave and how they are able to manage at the edge without losing their footing; *Competing on the Edge: Strategy as Structured Chaos* (Boston: Harvard Business School Press, 1998). Likewise, Peter Senge was an early proponent of creating learning organizations that scan widely, and many of the characteristics he identified apply here; *The Fifth Discipline* (New York: Doubleday/Currency, 1990).

16. The philosopher C. West Churchman has examined how deeply embedded philosophical premises influence the inquiring systems organizations build; *The Design of Inquiring Systems* (New York: Basic Books, 1971). Mason and Mitroff extended this work by examining how managers' personalities and psychological styles (as measured, for instance, using the well-known Meyers-Briggs test) impact their preferences for data and inquiring systems; see R. D. Mason and I. I. Mitroff, "A Program for Research on Management Information Systems," *Management Science* 19, no. 5 (1973): 475–487. Anthropological research on organizational culture can further illuminate how values and norms may hamper or enhance peripheral vision. Organizations in which power distance is great, uncertainty avoidance is high, and future orientation is weak—to mention just three well-studied dimensions of

organizational culture—will probably perform poorly when confronted with weak signals from the periphery or from lower levels within the organization. For insights about organizational culture, see Geert Hofstede, *Culture's Consequences: International Differences in Work-Related Values* (Newbury Park, CA: Sage Publications, 1980); Robert J. House et al., eds., *Culture and Leadership in Organizations: The GLOBE Study of 62 Societies* (Beverly Hills, CA: Sage Publications, in press); Charles Hampden-Turner and Fons Trompenaars, *Building Cross-Cultural Competence: How to Create Wealth from Conflicting Values* (New Haven, CT: Yale University Press, 2000).

17. "A Golden Vein," *The Economist*, June 10 2004, 22–23.

18. Ronald S. Burt, *Structural Holes* (Cambridge, MA: Harvard University Press, 1992); see also John Seely Brown and Paul Duguid, *The Social Life of Information* (Boston: Harvard Business School Press, 2002).

19. Duvall and Nash, "Mattel."

20. Youngme Moon and John A. Quelch, "Starbucks: Delivering Customer Service," Case 9-504-016 (Boston: Harvard Business School, 2004).

21. James Surowiecki, *Wisdom of Crowds: Why the Many Are Smarter than the Few and How Collective Wisdom Shapes Business, Economies, Societies, and Nations* (New York: Doubleday, 2004).

22. Chuck Salter, "Ivy Ross Is Not Playing Around," *Fast Company*, November 2004, 104.

*Chapter 8*

1. From a speech given by Lord John Browne at Bradford University on November 23, 2001; for the full text of the speech, see www.bp.com/genericarticle.do?categoryId=98&contentId=2000350.

2. Sources include Office of Communications, *The Communications Market 2004—Overview*, August 11, 2004; BBC *Annual Report of Accounts*, 2003/2004; Department for Culture, Media and Sport, *Review of the BBC's Royal Charter, A Strong BBC, Independent of Government*, March 2005; BBC, *Building Public Value; Reviewing the BBC for a Digital World* (undated); "With One Bound, Auntie Was Free," *The Economist*, March 3, 2005, 55.

3. The terms "minding" and "mining" were used in a presentation by John Seely Brown at the Wharton conference on Peripheral Vision, May 2003, and in his subsequent article "Minding and Mining the Periphery," *Long Range Planning* 37 (2004): 143–151.

4. "Change and Reorganisation—Signs of Things to Come as Thompson Becomes DG," BBC, June 22, 2004, www.bbc.co.uk/pressoffice/pressreleases/stories/2004/06_june/22/thompson.shtml.

5. "BBC Launches Its Vision of the Future and Manifesto for Action," BBC Press Releases, June 29, 2004, www.bbc.co.uk/pressoffice/pressreleases/stories/2004/06_june/29/bpv.shtml.

6. Our approach to the periphery is complementary to Max H. Bazerman and Michael D. Watkins, *Predictable Surprises: The Disasters You Should Have Seen Com-*

ing and How to Prevent Them (Boston: Harvard Business School Press, 2004), 1. They focus on the more predictable end of the continuum of uncertainty and offer valuable insights into why events can take an organization by surprise "despite prior knowledge of all the information needed to anticipate the event and the consequences." We begin further toward the unpredictable end of the spectrum and then build a capability for taking early action on signals of threats and opportunities.

7. We are using *tolerable* in the sense of the second level of residual uncertainty, as defined by Hugh Courtney, *20:20 Foresight: Crafting Strategy in an Uncertain World* (Boston: Harvard Business School Press, 2001), chap. 2.

8. In a recent white paper, Scott Snyder and Paul J. H. Schoemaker create a template for such a radar system. It describes how to develop systems and metrics for expanding dashboards to embrace uncertainties, test assumptions, and understand weak signals in the context of scenarios; "Strategic Action Radar: A Scenario-Based Tracking System to Sense and Adapt to a Changing World," white paper, Decision Strategies International, November 2004.

9. George S. Day, *The Market-Driven Organization: Understanding, Attracting, and Keeping Valuable Customers* (New York: Free Press, 1999); "Creating a Market Driven Organization," *Sloan Management Review* 41, no. 1 (Fall 1999): 11–22.

10. Gary Hamel, *Leading the Revolution* (Boston: Harvard Business School Press, 2000).

*Appendix A*

1. D. T. Cambell and D. M. Fiske, "Convergent and Discriminant Validation by the Multitrait-Multimethod Matrix," *Psychological Bulletin* 56 (1959): 81–105.

*Appendix B*

1. This appendix builds on a previous article by the authors, "Driving Through the Fog: Managing at the Edge," *Long Range Planning*, special issue on *Peripheral Vision: Sensing and Acting on Weak Signals* 37, no. 2 (April 2004): 117–121. (The authors also edited this special issue.)

2. Some scholars have examined the issue of the periphery and tried to link it to overall performance, for example, R. L. Daft, J. Jormunen, and D. Parks, "Chief Executive Scanning, Environmental Characteristics and Company Performance: An Empirical Study," *Strategic Management Journal* 9 (1988): 123–139.

3. We view our approach as similar to the way prescriptive advice developed in the field of decision sciences—descriptive models were combined with normative models, such as expected utility theory, to guide the development of more practical prescriptive approaches; see Paul Kleindorfer, Howard C. Kunreuther, and Paul J. H. Schoemaker, *Decision Sciences: An Integrative Perspective* (Cambridge, UK: Cambridge University Press, 1993).

4. Although researchers have had difficulty defining and studying organizational learning, there is a reasonable acceptance of the information processing view adopted here, which goes back to Richard M. Cyert and James G. March, *A Behavioral Theory of the Firm* (Englewood Cliffs, NJ: Prentice-Hall, 1963). See also

Barbara Levitt and James G. March, "Organizational Learning," *Annual Review of Sociology* 14, (1988): 319–340; K. Imai, I. Nonaka, and H. Takeuchi, "Managing the New Product Development Process: How Japanese Firms Learn and Unlearn," in *The Uneasy Alliance*, ed. K. Clark, R. Hayes, and C. Lorenz (Boston: Harvard Business School Press, 1985), 337–376; George Huber, "Organizational Learning: The Contributing Processes and Literature," *Organization Science* 2 (1991): 88–115.

5. Alan Newell and Herbert Simon, *Human Problem Solving* (Englewood Cliffs, NJ: Prentice Hall, 1972). See also Herbert Simon, *Sciences of the Artificial* (Cambridge, MA: MIT Press, 1969); David A. Garvin, "Building a Learning Organization," *Harvard Business Review*, July–August 1993, 78–91; Karl E. Weick, *Sensemaking in Organizations* (Thousand Oaks, CA: Sage Publications, 1995).

6. James G. March and Herbert A. Simon, *Organizations* (New York: John Wiley, 1958); Richard M. Cyert and James G. March, *A Behavioral Theory of the Firm* (Englewood Cliffs, NJ: Prentice Hall, 1963); James G. March, *Decisions and Organizations* (New York: Blackwell, 1988).

7. James D. Thompson, *Organizations in Action* (New York: McGraw-Hill, 1967); D. Steinbruner, *The Cybernatic Theory of Decisions* (Princeton, NJ: Princeton University Press, 1974); Jay Galbraith, *Designing Complex Organizations* (Reading, MA: Addison-Wesley, 1973), and *Designing Organizations* (San Francisco: Jossey-Bass, 2002).

8. George P. Huber, "Organizational Learning: The Contributing Process and Literatures," *Organization Science* 2 (February 1991): 88–115.

9. Roy Lachman, Janet L. Lachman, and Earl C. Butterfield, *Cognitive Psychology and Information Processing* (New York: John Wiley & Sons, 1979).

10. To fully acknowledge the contributions of Daniel Kahneman and Amos Tversky is beyond the scope of this book. However, their most important papers and many related ones by students and colleagues are gathered in Daniel Kahneman and Amos Tversky, eds., *Choices, Values, and Frames* (New York: Cambridge University Press/Russell Sage Foundation, 2000). Their earlier work, also with related papers of interest, is collected in Daniel Kahneman, Paul Slovic, and Amos Tversky, eds., *Judgment Under Uncertainty: Heuristics and Biases* (New York: Cambridge University Press, 1982).

11. The emphasis on developing learning cultures in organizations was pioneered by Peter Senge in his well-known book, *The Fifth Discipline* (New York: Currency/Doubleday, 1990). For a shorter version, see Peter Senge, "The Leader's New Work: Building Learning Organizations," *Sloan Management Review* 32 (Fall 1990): 7–23; and for elaborated essays, see Sarita Chawla and John Renesch, *Learning Organizations: Developing Cultures for Tomorrow's Workplace* (Portland, OR: Productivity Press, 1995). The strategic significance of learning—especially about the future—is further underscored in Gary Hamel and C. K. Prahalad, *Competing for the Future* (Boston: Harvard Business School Press, 1994). Organizational obstacles to learning and change are addressed by Chris Argyris, *Strategy, Change, and Defensive Routines* (Boston: Pitman Publishing, 1985). In the realm of new technologies, these

obstacles loom especially large, as shown by Clayton M. Christensen, *The Innovator's Dilemma* (Boston: Harvard Business School Press, 1997).

12. John D. W. Morecroft and John D. Sterman, *Modeling for Learning Organizations* (Portland, OR: Productivity Press, 1994). An integrated treatment of dynamic systems modeling is offered in John D. Sterman, *Business Dynamics: Systems Thinking and Modeling for a Complex World* (Columbus, OH: McGraw-Hill/Irwin, 2000). For more on mental models, see Rob Ranyard, *Decision Making: Cognitive Models and Explanations* (New York: Routledge, 1997); Robert Axelrod, ed., *The Structure of Decision: The Cognitive Maps of Political Elites* (Princeton: Princeton University Press, 1976); Josh Klayman and Paul J. H. Schoemaker, "Thinking About the Future: A Cognitive Perspective," *Journal of Forecasting* 12 (1993): 161–168. The classic references to mental models and their cognitive functions are Dedre Gentner and Albert L. Stevens, eds., *Mental Models* (Hillsdale, NJ: Laurence Erlbaum Associates, 1983); Philip N. Johnson-Laird, *Mental Models*, 2nd ed. (Cambridge, MA: Harvard University Press, 1983).

13. The classic paper on decision making under conditions of ambiguity is Daniel Ellsberg, "Risk, Ambiguity, and the Savage Axioms," *Quarterly Journal of Economics* 75 (1961): 643–669, which is based on his seminal doctoral dissertation, recently republished (with an extensive new introduction by Isaac Levi) as *Risk, Ambiguity, and Decision* (New York: Garland, 2001). Decisions with unknown probabilities have been studied by many, including Hillel J. Einhorn and Robin M. Hogarth, "Decision Making Under Ambiguity," *Journal of Business* 59, no. 4, pt. 2 (1986): S225–255; M. Cohen, J. Jaffray, and T. Said, "Individual Behavior Under Risk and Under Uncertainty: An Experimental Study," *Theory and Decisions* 18 (1985): 203–228; Paul J. H. Schoemaker, "Choices Involving Uncertain Probabilities: Tests of Generalized Utility Models," *Journal of Economic and Organizational Behavior* 16 (1991): 295–317.

14. George Stigler, "The Economics of Information," *Journal of Political Economy* 69 (1961), 213–225.

15. Jack Hirshleifer and John G. Riley, *The Analytics of Uncertainty and Information, Cambridge Surveys of Economic Literature* (Cambridge, UK: Cambridge University Press, 1992).

16. For a more extensive description of this tool, see Paul J. H. Schoemaker, "Scenario Planning: A Tool for Strategic Thinking," *Sloan Management Review* 36 (Winter 1995): 25–40. For a conceptual and behavioral perspective, see Paul J. H. Schoemaker, "Multiple Scenario Developing: Its Conceptual and Behavioral Basis," *Strategic Management Journal* 14 (1993): 193–213. For managerial scenario applications, see Peter Schwartz, *The Art of the Long View* (New York: Doubleday, 1991); Kees van der Heijden, *Scenarios: The Art of Strategic Conversation* (New York: John Wiley, 1996); G. Ringland, *Scenario Planning* (New York: John Wiley, 1998); Liam Fahey and Robert M. Randall, eds., *Learning from the Future* (New York: John Wiley, 1998); Paul J. H. Schoemaker, *Profiting from Uncertainty: Strategies for Succeeding No Matter What the Future Brings* (New York: Free Press, 2002).

17. James G. March, "Exploration and Exploitation in Organizational Learning," *Organizational Learning* 2 (February 1991): 71–87.

18. Senge, *The Fifth Discipline*.

19. The case for having prior hypotheses is persuasively made by James M. Utterback and James W. Brown, "Monitoring for Technological Opportunities," *Business Horizons* 15 (October 1971): 5–15.

20. George S. Day, *The Market-Driven Organization: Understanding, Attracting, and Keeping Valuable Customers* (New York: Free Press, 1999), especially chap. 5.

21. Gerald Zaltman, *How Customers Think: Essential Insights into the Mind of the Market* (Boston: Harvard Business School Press, 2003).

22. Bernard Jaworski and Ajay K. Kohli, "Market Orientation: Antecedents and Consequences," *Journal of Marketing* 57 (July 1993): 53–70; John C. Narver and Stanley F. Slater, "The Effect of Market Orientation on Business Profitability," *Journal of Marketing* 54 (October 1990): 20–35. For a recent synthesis of this work, see Rohit Deshpandé and John U. Farley, "Measuring Market Orientation," *Journal of Market-Focused Management* 2 (1998): 213–232; John Narver and Stanley Slater, "Additional Thoughts on the Measurement of Market Orientation: A Comment on Deshpandé and Farley," *Journal of Market-Focused Management* 2 (1998): 233–236.

23. These results are derived from George S. Day and Prakash Nedungadi, "Managerial Representations of Competitive Advantage," *Journal of Marketing* 58 (April 1994): 40, by applying the results of subjective judgments of relative financial performance to the distributions of return on investment results in the Pacific Institute for the Mathematical Sciences (PIMS) database. We caution that the performance differences do *not* control for differences in the competitive market environment or strategic choices. These profitability results are in line with results in John C. Narver and Stanley F. Slater, "The Effect of a Market Orientation on Business Profitability," *Journal of Marketing* 54 (October 1990): 20–35, which uses a different procedure for measuring market orientation.

24. See Liam Fahey, *Competitors: Outwitting, Outmaneuvering, and Outperforming* (New York: John Wiley, 1999); Leonard M. Fuld, *The New Competitor Intelligence: The Complete Resource for Finding, Analyzing and Using Information About Your Competitors* (New York: John Wiley, 1994); John E. Prescott and Stephen H. Miller, eds., *Proven Strategies in Competitive Intelligence: Lessons from the Trenches* (New York: John Wiley, 2000). The role of complements gained wide visibility with Adam M. Brandenberger and Barry H. Nalebuff, *Co-Opetition* (New York: Doubleday, 1996).

25. George S. Day and Paul J. H. Schoemaker, eds., *Wharton on Managing Emerging Technologies* (New York: John Wiley & Sons, 2000).

26. Don S. Doering and Roche Parayre, "Assessing Technologies," in *Wharton on Managing Emerging Technologies*, 75–98.

27. Constantinos C. Markides and Paul A. Geroski, *Fast Second: How Smart Companies Bypass Radical Innovation to Enter and Dominate New Markets* (San Francisco: Jossey-Bass, 2004).

28. Howard Raiffa, *Decision Analysis: Introductory Lectures on Choices Under Uncertainty* (Reading, MA: Addison-Wesley, 1968).

29. Probe and learn is most akin to the useful typology for uncertain environments, strategies, and actions under uncertainty developed by Courtney and coworkers at McKinsey of "reserving the right to play," whereas sensing and following or leading may both be shaping strategies. H. Courtney, J. Kirkland, and P. Viguerie, "Strategy Under Uncertainty," *Harvard Business Review*, November–December 1997, 67–79.

30. For more on real options, see William F. Hamilton and Graham R. Mitchell, "Managing R&D as a Strategic Option," *Research Technology Management* 31 (May–June 1988): 15–22; Edward H. Bowman and Dileep Hurry, "Strategy Through the Options Lens: An Integrated View of Resource Investments and the Incremental-Choice Process," *Academy of Management Review* 18 (1993): 760–782; Rita G. McGrath, "A Real Options Logic for Initiation Technology Positioning Investments," *Academy of Management Review* 22 (1997): 974–996; Ian C. MacMillan and Rita Gunther McGrath, "Crafting R&D Project Portfolios," *Research Technology Management* 45 (September–October 2002): 48–59.

31. Numerous excellent books on creativity can be consulted for more specific techniques. See, in particular, such classics as Paul Watzlawick, John H. Weakland, and Richard Fisch, *Change: Principles of Problem Formulation and Problem Resolution* (New York: W. W. Norton, 1974); James L. Adams, *Conceptual Blockbusting* (Reading, MA: Addison Wesley Longman, 1986); Edward de Bono, *Lateral Thinking: Creativity Step by Step* (New York: Harper & Row, 1973); Roger van Oech, *A Whack on the Side of the Head: How You Can Be More Creative*, rev. ed. (New York: Warner Books, 1998), which even comes with a Wack Pack of cards. For creativity in an organizational context, see Robert Lawrence Kuhn, ed., *Handbook for Creative and Innovative Managers* (New York: McGraw-Hill, 1987); Jane Henry, ed., *Creative Management* (London, UK: Sage Publications, 1991); Alan G. Robinson and Sam Stern, *Corporate Creativity* (San Francisco: Berrett-Koehler Publishers, 1998), 9–11. For a comparison of techniques, see Kenneth R. MacCrimmon and Christian Wagner, "Stimulating Ideas Through Creativity Software," *Management Science* 40, no. 11 (November 1994): 1514–1532.

32. The concept of capabilities is not new; it dates back to Edith T. Penrose, *The Theory of the Growth Firm* (London: Basil Blackwell, 1959). Its recent popularity can be traced to C. K. Prahalad and Gary Hamel, "The Core Competence of the Corporation," *Harvard Business Review*, May–June 1990, 79–91. For academic background on the resource-based view of strategy, see J. Barney, "Firm Resources and Sustained Competitive Advantage," *Journal of Management* 17, no. 1, (1991): 99–120; R. Amit and Paul J. H. Schoemaker, "Strategic Assets and Organizational Rent," *Strategic Management Journal* 14, no. 1 (1993): 33–46. D. J. Teece, G. Pisano, and A. Shuen, "Dynamic Capabilities and Strategic Management," *Strategic Management Journal* 18, no. 7 (1997): 509–533. For our purposes, the concepts competency and capability are interchangeable, although we prefer to reserve the notion of core competencies for cross-corporation purposes and capabilities for within-business-unit purposes. See George S. Day, "The Capabilities of Market-Driven Organizations," *Journal of Marketing* 58 (October 1994): 37–52.

33. Kathleen Eisenhardt, Stanford University, has studied, with colleagues, how firms operating in high-velocity environments behave and how they are able to manage at the edge without losing their footing; see *Competing on the Edge: Strategy as Structured Chaos* (Boston: Harvard Business School Press, 1998). Peter Senge (in *The Fifth Discipline*) likewise was an early proponent of creating learning organizations that scan widely, and many of the characteristics he identified apply here.

34. David DeLong and Liam Fahey, "Building the Knowledge Based Organization: How Culture Drives Knowledge Behaviors," Ernst & Young Center for Business Innovation, May 1997.

35. Rohit Deshpandé, John U. Farley, and Frederick E. Webster Jr., "Corporate Culture, Customer Orientation, and Innovativeness in Japanese Firms: A Quadrad Analysis," *Journal of Marketing* 53 (January 1993): 3–15, and "Factors Affecting Organizational Performance: A Five-Country Comparison," Marketing Science Institute report, 97–108, May 1997. Their model is adapted from Robert E. Quinn and J. Rohrbaugh, "A Spatial Model of Effectiveness Criteria: Toward a Competing Values Approach to Organizational Analysis," *Management Science* 29 (1983): 363–377, and it is described in Richard W. Woodman and W. A. Passmore, eds., *Research in Organizational Change and Development*, vol. 5 (Greenwich, CT: JAI Press, 1991). We also employed some of the concepts in Paul McDonald and Geoffrey Gantz, "Getting Value from Shared Values," *Organizational Dynamics* (1994): 64–77.

36. Clayton M. Christensen, *The Innovator's Dilemma* (Boston: Harvard Business School Press, 1997); Andrew S. Grove, *Only the Paranoid Survive* (New York: Currency, 1996); Richard Foster and Sarah Kaplan, *Creative Destruction* (New York: Currency, 2001).

37. Malcolm Gladwell, *The Tipping Point* (Boston: Little, Brown, 2000).

38. Wayne Burkan, *Wide Angle Vision* (New York: John Wiley, 1996); Ben Gilad, *Early Warning* (New York: AMACOM, 2004); Jim Harris, *Blindsided: How To Spot the Next Breakthrough that Will Change Your Business* (Oxford: Capstone, 2002).

39. Chun Wei Choo, *Information Management for the Intelligent Organization: The Art of Scanning the Environment* (Medford, NJ: Information Today, 1995); Karl E. Weick, *Sensemaking in Organizations* (Thousand Oaks, CA: Sage Publications, 1995); Karl E. Weick and Kathleen M. Sutcliffe, *Managing the Unexpected* (San Francisco: Jossey-Bass, 2001).

40. Haridimos Tsoukas and Jill Shepherd, eds., *Managing the Future: Foresight in the Knowledge Economy* (Malden, MA: Blackwell, 2004).

41. Timothy Naftali, *Blind Spot: The Secret History of American Counterterrorism* (New York: Basic Books, 2005).

42. Clayton M. Christensen, Scott D. Anthony, and Erik A. Roth, *Seeing What's Next* (Boston: Harvard Business School Press, 2004).

43. Max H. Bazerman and Michael D. Watkins, *Predictable Surprises: The Disasters You Should Have Seen Coming and How to Prevent Them* (Boston: Harvard Business School Press, 2004); W. Chan Kim and Renée Mauborgne, *Blue Ocean Strategy* (Boston: Harvard Business School Press, 2005).

44. Jerry Wind and Colin Crook, *The Power of Impossible Thinking* (Upper Saddle River, NJ: Wharton School Publishing, 2004).

*Appendix C*

1. This discussion is drawn from the work of Claus Bundesen and colleagues, who describe the basic process of visual attention as follows:

> A normal perceptual cycle consists of two waves: a wave of unselected processing followed by a wave of selected processing. During the first wave, cortical processing resources are distributed at random (unselectively) across the visual field. At the end of the first wave, an attentional weight has been computed for each object in the visual field and stored in a saliency map. The weights are used for reallocation of attention (visual processing capacity) by dynamic remapping of the receptive field's cortical neurons such that the number of neurons allocated to an object increases with the attentional weight of the object. Hence, during the second wave, cortical processing is selective in the sense that the amount of processing resources (number of neurons) allocated to an object depends on the attentional weight of the object. Because more processing resources are devoted to behaviorally important objects than less important ones, the important objects are more likely to become encoded into visual short-term memory (VSTM). The VSTM system is conceived as a (K-winners-take-all) feedback mechanism that sustains activity in the neurons that have won the attentional competition. (Claus Bundesen, Thomas Habekost, and Soren Kyllingsbaek, "A Neural Theory of Visual Attention: Bridging Cognition and Neurophysiology," *Psychological Review* 112, no. 2 [2005]: 292.)

2. Douglas B. Light, *The Senses* (Philadelphia: Chelsea House, 2004).

# Acknowledgments

We are indebted to numerous people who helped us in developing this multidisciplinary book, from students to colleagues to business leaders and editors. We cannot acknowledge them all here, but do wish to thank some by name.

The impetus for our book was a conference we organized in May of 2003 on the topic "Peripheral Vision." It was sponsored by Wharton School's Mack Center for Technological Innovation and brought together a distinguished group of executives and thought leaders. The speakers included such noted academics as C. K. Prahalad (University of Michigan) and Sidney Winter (Wharton), as well as John Seely Brown (Xerox Parc), Richard Foster (McKinsey), Steve Haeckle (IBM), Larry Huston (Procter & Gamble), and Anil Menon (IBM) from the business community.

During this conference we were encouraged and invited by Charles Baden-Fuller, editor-in-chief of *Long Range Planning*, to develop a special issue on the subject. We accepted, and the ensuing effort further drew our attention to managerial questions about the periphery, culminating in an edited volume titled *Special Issue on Peripheral Vision, Long Range Planning*, edited by George S. Day and Paul J. H. Schoemaker (April 2004).

We received valuable managerial feedback on early book drafts from Paul's colleagues at Decision Strategies International, notably Michael Mavaddat, Franck Schuurmans, Bernardo Sichel, and Scott Snyder. Also, various academic colleagues kindly provided commentary, including attendees of the University of Chicago's Center for Decision Research, where Paul presented the conceptual framework. Special mention should be made of Russ Ackoff, Liam Fahey, Reid Hasty, Josh Klayman, John Lord, and Richard Shell.

We also benefited greatly from feedback offered by various managers and executives, including three excellent anonymous reviewers secured by the Harvard Business School Press. We received insightful executive commentary from Tom Graham (Kinecta) and Govi Rao (Philips Lighting) on the entire manuscript, as well as crucial background information on various case examples from John Allison (Branch Banking and Trust Company), Dr. Robert Bailey (Wills Eye Center), John Carmon (Carmon Community Funeral Homes), Harvey Hartman (Hartman Group), Vince Melchiorre (Tasty Baking), Sally Osman (BBC), and John Ranieri (DuPont).

We are especially grateful to Robert E. Gunther who tirelessly rewrote each chapter multiple times in good cheer and with a keen mind. Robert managed to move his family across the country (and back) during the writing process while somehow finding the time and dedication to take this book to a much higher plateau than we could have alone. Whatever merit the book's prose and style have, most of it is due to Robert, who became our friend and intellectual companion as we worked our way through various concepts, frameworks, and examples. Robert forced us to clarify our own thinking and make it relevant to managers while adding valuable insights and examples himself as well.

We also received valuable editorial advice from Kirsten Sandberg, a highly respected and seasoned editor of the Harvard Business School Press who is true master of metaphors. She recognized the book's potential early on and kindly visited us in Philadelphia to convey her enthusiasm. Kirsten volunteered much-needed editorial advice about both the metaphor and the approach. It was Kirsten's infectious belief and strong support for the book that propelled us to team up with Harvard Business School Press, which has done an outstanding job bringing this book into print. We thank all involved, including Gardiner Morse for his indirect advice.

We also wish to recognize the important role that the Mack Center for Technological Innovation (generously endowed by William and Phyllis Mack) played in our research and writings. In addition, we received annual funding from our industry partners and obtained wise council from our core group colleagues, namely Raffi Amit, Terry Fadem, Bill Hamilton, Harbir Singh, Jitendra Singh, Michael Tomczyk, and Sid Winter. The genesis of our book lies in the enthusiastic endorsements of this group when we proposed peripheral vision as a possible conference topic in 2002.

Last, we acknowledge the vibrant intellectual climate of the Wharton School and its surrounding University of Pennsylvania for providing a stimulating environment for research and learning. We were fortunate to test and develop our ideas during numerous workshops and executive development sessions at Wharton. We thank all for their insights and support while taking full responsibility for any shortcoming this book may have.

# Index

# About the Authors

*George S. Day* is the Geoffrey T. Boisi Professor of Marketing and codirector of the Mack Center for Technological Innovation at the Wharton School of the University of Pennsylvania. His research and teaching interests center on marketing, the management of technological innovations, strategic planning, organizational change, and competitive strategies in global markets.

Prior to joining the Wharton School faculty, he taught at Stanford University, IMD in Lausanne, Switzerland, and the University of Toronto, and he was executive director of the Marketing Science Institute, an industry-supported research consortium.

Day has published fifteen books, including *Wharton on Managing Emerging Technologies*, with Paul Schoemaker, and *Market-Driven Strategy*. His publications have received numerous awards, and he has received the Charles Coolidge Parlin and Converse Awards for outstanding contributions to the field of marketing and the Academy of Marketing Science and AMA/Irwin/McGraw-Hill Distinguished Marketing Educator Award.

He serves as a consultant to many of the world's leading corporations and is a member of private-sector, public-sector, and foundation boards of directors. He currently resides in Bryn Mawr, Pennsylvania.

*Paul J. H. Schoemaker* is founder, chairman, and CEO of Decision Strategies International (www.thinkdsi.com). He also serves as research director of the Mack Center for Technological Innovation at Wharton, where he teaches strategy and decision making. Formerly, he was a professor in the Graduate School of Business at the University of Chicago and a visiting professor for Cedep at Insead, France.

His interests are in strategic management, decision theory, organizational decision making, and emerging technologies. Schoemaker has written several books, including *Winning Decisions* (with J. Edward Russo) and *Profiting from Uncertainty*. His work has appeared in journals such as the *Harvard Business Review*, *Strategic Management Journal*, *Management Science*, and the *Journal of Economic Literature*. His writings have been published in over ten languages.

Schoemaker frequently gives seminars on decision making and strategic thinking to executives in Europe, America, and the Far East. He has taught in the executive programs of University of California at Berkeley, Columbia University, Cedep at

Insead (France), Cornell University, University of Chicago, and the Wharton School at the University of Pennsylvania. ISI ranked Schoemaker in the top 1 percent of researchers cited in academic business and economics journals. He was also the recipient of the prestigious Best Paper Award of the Strategic Management Society.

Schoemaker serves on the board of several profit and nonprofit organizations, including the Decision Education Foundation. He has also been an active investor in new technology ventures. He enjoys tennis, golf, and piano and lives with his wife in Villanova, Pennsylvania.